European Costumed Dolls

by Polly and Pam Judd

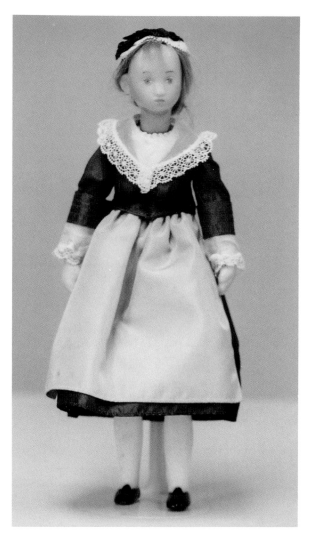

Illustration 1: **Sasha Doll** from Zürich, Switzerland.
SEE: *Illustration 1, Page 5.*

Published by Hobby House Press, Inc.
Grantsville, Maryland 21536

Dedication

This book is dedicated to Wally Judd Jr., Donna Judd, Eryn Judd, and Kyle Judd. They have shared our lives and love of traveling. Now it is their turn to see the world.

Acknowledgements

Many people have shared their pictures and expertise with us as we have written this book. We want to thank Barbara and Jim Comienski, Shirley Karaba, and Sandra Strater who have spent many hours in research and photography.

The "After Dark Doll Club" is especially interested in the dolls of the world, and we thank them for their enthusiastic research meetings which often involve the regional, historical and unusual dolls and toys which might easily be forgotten.

Mary Elizabeth Poole always manages to find "that special doll" for which we have been searching.

We want to express our deep appreciation of the following people who sent photographs or helped us in other ways: Lois Jean Adam, Laverne Ahrens, Beverly Findley, Nancy Bakes, Jeanne Bakes, Ester Borgis, Carlton Brown, Dee Cermak, Nancy Gallaher, Joe Golembieski, Shari Gordon, Jean Horton, Lois Janner, Laverne Kotty, Ana Leben, Kathy Lincoln, McMasters Productions, Patricia Moisuk, Patricia Parton, Michael Policopf, Thelma Purvis, Louise Schnell, Anita Sigust, Kathleen Smith, Nancy Smith, Mary Tanner, Ann Votaw, Christopher Walmsley.

Additional copies of this book may be purchased at $14.95 from
HOBBY HOUSE PRESS, INC.
1 Corporate Drive
Grantsville, Maryland 21536
1-800-554-1447
(please add $4.75 per copy for postage)
or from your favorite bookstore or dealer.

ISBN: 0-87588-426-1

Table of Contents

Other Identification and Value Guides in this Series:

Asian & African Costumed Dolls, 2nd in series
The Americas and Pacific Areas Costumed Dolls, 3rd in series

Whenever possible the author uses a regional reference. Country names and boundaries were correct at the time of printing. It is possible that these names and boundaries may have changed since the time of printing due to the evolution of the world.

Forward

International, provincial, and regional costume dolls have always been popular with collectors. Many of the early doll authors featured these colorful dolls in their books. The authors are grateful for this early research. We are also grateful for the many current collectors who have urged us to write these books and shared pictures of their dolls for future generations to enjoy.

This is the first of a trilogy of books about dolls from around the world. In our wide travels we have found that natives no longer wear the traditional costumes daily, but wear "pants and tops" much like we do in our everyday life. However, we have illustrated in this book the old costume heritages of European fairs, festivals, dance and music competitions.

For the authors the love of these dolls started when Pam was five, and our Christmas tree was decorated with colorful dolls her grandmother brought from her travels. We still follow this tradition. This is now our heritage and that of our son and brother and his children. It has been our turn to travel extensively, and we have pursued both the usual and the unusual dolls to bring home with us.

We have both been social studies teachers for many years, and have experienced the excitement of children actually "seeing and understanding" people from all over the world better through these dolls.

We have been in a doll museum in Taiwan where they have a large display of their own historical dolls as well as dolls from other parts of the world. They try to get most of the school children to this museum sometime in their school years. It is not just the Americans who are interested in "keeping" the heritage of the world. It was fun to see the American Alexander and Barbie dolls from this Taiwanese perspective.

The second book will include Asia and African dolls. The last book will include "the rest" of the world. We invite our readers from both the United States and other countries to help us by sending letters and information to us in care of Hobby House Press.

Our objectives in this book are to identify the many different European ethnic or regional costumes, doll materials, and artistic talents that are used in various countries and in various time periods. However, most of all we want to show both the expensive and the inexpensive dolls. This type of collecting is for everyone who loves the people around the world.

System Used for Pricing Dolls

International dolls have been on the market from early historical times. In early years, ships that sailed the seas used dolls to barter. Today, most travelers bring home dolls from other countries as presents for their children, grandchildren and friends.

Unfortunately many of the expensive bisque dolls have been redressed and no longer wear their original clothes. Luck-

ily the less expensive dolls usually end up with their original clothes intact. Collectors of these dolls are fortunate because most of them were "shelf" dolls and are often in excellent condition.

Previous to World War II and immediately after, International dolls were highly sought through doll dealers such as Kimport, Krug, and the Wide World Doll Club. The interest in these companies waned as more people traveled around the world.

However, today there are various interest and ethnic groups that see a changing world becoming very similar everywhere, and they are forming organizations to help save their heritage. This has increased the prices of these dolls. Considering the workmanship, at this moment in time they are a "bargain." But as the authors sought to verify prices in the last year during the writing of this book, we have seen a slight increase.

The range of prices given for each doll includes good-to-mint condition with all-original clothes. Tissue-mint in the box dolls, will command higher prices and dolls in poor condition will be about one third to one half of the lowest price.

The prices of individual dolls have been gathered from dealers and customers from coast-to-coast. Auction prices have been monitored and international prices have been considered. While local prices vary, they do not vary as much as with most of the other types of dolls.

At auction, unheralded rare dolls do bring remarkable prices. However, dolls that are presumed to be rare have a way of appearing after a book is published, and as in the case of this book, when the doll has been identified. With this occurrence collectors and dealers will have to adjust to an upward price scale.

Swiss Zürich Sasha Doll: 19.75in (27cm); doll made from a form of dental plastic of the period; plastic shoulder plate so head can rotate; cloth body with firm stuffing; strawberry blonde hair; clothing has all natural fibers; lace-trimmed pantaloons and slip; maroon taffeta skirt; tight fitted and detailed jacket with lace trimmed fichau overlaps; white blouse; black "mob" cap; white blouse; yellow apron; painted white stockings and black shoes; 1958.

The owner has done research about Sasha dolls in Switzerland, and she finds that there were only about 100 of these dolls made. The dentist ran out of material, and Sasha was not happy with the dolls. The dolls were sold at the Heimatwerk, a national chain of Swiss Handicraft shops still in existence.

Working on this doll were both Sasha and K. Glunk. Both painted the faces of individual dolls, so not all dolls are alike. Those painted by Sasha (and for other original Sasha dolls) were done after the doll was dressed so Sasha could "pull together" the costumes, the hair, the eyes and other features. This doll has green eyes to pick up the yellow highlighted colors from the costume and hair. Her pupils are asymmetrical, one side not exactly duplicating the other giving her a pensive look. This, too, was typical of other dolls hand painted by Sasha. The Glunk dolls did not have the same style of painting.

This is a Festtracht or holiday costume from Zürich. This is a rare doll and only a few have surfaced.

MARKS: None on this doll, but the owner has seen another such doll with a tag.

SEE: *Illustration 1. Ann Votaw Collection* (see page 1 for photograph).

AUSTRIA

Austria was once the proud center of the Austria-Hungarian Hapsburg Empire with a history of dominance for 1000 years. During that long period there were many additions and subtractions to the various provinces. Today it is a modern country retaining its long love affair with the arts, excellent cuisine, wine, and dolls.

The old costumes and dolls of the provinces reflect the different populations that were once part of that empire, and they also reflect the differing topography, the artistic life, music, and beauty of a country which still allows its citizens leisure time to enjoy various activities.

Like all of the countries of Europe, the Austrian costumes vary not only from province to province, but from city to city, village to village, and family to family. Each puts a different twist to the basic design.

REGIONS
1. Vienna
2. Eastern Austria: Burgenland, most of Styria, and a small section of Niederîsterreich.
3. The Danube Valley: Niederösterreich, another small section of Niederösterreich, a small portion of Oberösterreich, Linz the third largest city, and Weinviertel.
4. The Lake District: Upper Austria, a small portion of Salzburg Province, and Styria.
5. Salzburg.
6. Carinthia Province
7. Eastern Alps: East Tirol (Tyrol), part of Salzburg Province, West Styria.
8. Western Alps: Innsbruck, Tirol (Tyrol), Vorarlberg, Montafon.

Austrian-Dolls of the Tyrol

The Tyrol is the central mountainous area of the European continent. Along with Austria, it includes parts of Southern Germany, Switzerland, Lichtenstein, and Northern Italy. These areas share a common culture, similar costumes, and often the same language (German).

Within this region there are differences in customs an dress. Often the styles show great individuality. In general women wear blouses covered by buttoned or tied bodices or vests, full skirts, and large, ornate headdresses. Silver is important for buttons and jewelry.

The men wear both short or long jackets, scarves, and prefer knee-length dark breeches. Occasionally they wear the shorter "lederhosen." "Trachen" is a word for the Tyrolean clothes.

Dolls follow the same pattern of dress, and if the doll is not marked it is difficult to tell the difference between Tyrolean and Bavarian. The Tyrolean older dolls often have real silver buttons, jewelry, and long silver chains. When polished, the dolls sparkle.

Austrian Woman: 9in (23cm) composition; picture shown in Romanian section (see *Illustration 186*, pages 122, 123); white apron with large white puffed sleeves; heavily embroidered top; red sash; blue print skirt; high leather shoes; before 1911.
MARKS: None.
SEE: *Illustration 186, page 123. McMasters Productions.*

Wachau Girl: She is visiting Lucerne, Switzerland. (see *Illustration 240*, page 153.)

WELCOME TO CHRISKINDELMARKET IN SALZBURG

Mozart, his sister, and the Tyrolean doll welcome you to the Christkindel Market in Salzburg. The wooden booths in the background are festive in greens from the forests, and each one is selling Christmas food, wine, beer, sausages, Christmas cookies, candy, handmade decorations, and dolls. These markets, situated in front of the main church or town square during the Christmas season, have centuries of tradition in both Austria and Germany. This picture was taken as the market was opening up in mid-morning. By mid-afternoon it will be packed with people. Budelfrau (Santa Claus figure) will be giving pony rides or listening to children. Dedt Moroz (Black Peter) armed with switches will be warning children to "be good".
Mozart (Doll on left): 9in (23cm); composition head; cloth body; painted face with "whistling mouth"; mohair wig; dressed in clothes of 18th century; orange felt coat with gold and black trim; black felt tricorn hat; lace jabot; aqua knee-length pants; pale lavender tapestry coat with gold and white ribbon trim; cotton stockings; felt shoes; all original; late 1980s.
MARKS: "BAITZ//Made in Austria//Mozart" on tag.

Pincushion (Doll in center): 6in (15cm); vinyl head; cloth body; Tyrolean style red felt dress and green apron; Black Tyrolean hat; white blouse; fastened to her waist with safety pins are four balls of thread; 1970s. *Sandra Strater Collection.*
MARKS: "HP//Helga//Made in Austria//Costume Dolls" on gold tag.
Mozart's Sister (Doll on right): 9in (23cm); composition head; cloth body; painted face with smiling mouth; mohair wig; dressed in clothes of the 18th century; blue cotton skirt with ruffle; yellow taffeta tapestry vest and pannier; lace collar and cuffs on sleeves; yellow felt hat trimmed with felt flowers; late 1980s.
MARKS: "BAITZ//Made in Austria//Mozart" on tag.
SEE: *Illustration 2, page 8.*

Innsbrook Dancing Couple: Both dolls 5in (13cm); cloth head; cloth body on armature; the boy has a typical Tyrolean outfit; the girl has a maroon skirt with a dainty white apron; small weskit; 1957.
MARKS: "Baitz//Made in Austria."
SEE: *Illustration 5, page 8. Thelma Purvis Collection.*

Vienna Lady: 12in (31cm); cloth needle sculpture; gray dress; blue velvet scarf; ribbon flowers; stovepipe-type hat; human hair wig.
MARKS: "Vienna" label stitched on doll.
SEE: *Illustration 6, page 7. Joe Golembieski Collection.*

Leni (Doll on left): 9.5in (24cm); European hard plastic head; cloth body; rose-colored skirt; gray brocade apron; white blouse decorated with gold braid; black Tyrolean hat trimmed with gold

braid; blond wig with pigtails rounded over ears. The Baitz dolls first had composition heads; later changing to hard plastic ones.

MARKS: "Baitz//Made in Austria//Leni" on heart-shaped tag.

Whistling Franzl (Doll in center): 9.5in (24cm); European hard plastic; cloth body; Tyrolean costume with black felt knees; high pants; red jacket with black lapels; white shirt; white and green embroidered belt; black felt Tyrolean hat; blonde hair; 1960s.

MARKS: "Baitz//Made in Austria//Franzl" on heart-shaped tag.

Lady in Black Dress (Doll on right): 9.5in (24cm); European hard plastic; cloth body; yellow apron; fancy decoration at neckline of dress; 1970s.

MARKS: "Baitz//Made in Austria" on front of tag; "Montafon" on back of tag; "Oesterreich" typed on a paper pinned to her dress under apron. **SEE:** *Illustration 4, page 8. Louise Schnell Collection.*

Tyrolean Boy (Doll on right): 18in (46cm); European composition; socket head; excellent color; five-piece composition body; glass eyes; open mouth with two teeth and tongue; thread hair; loden waistcoat with appliqued felt details; red collar and cuffs of sleeves; white shirt; brown wool pants; suspenders with felt applique; laced red ribbon on side of pants; wool shoes with red pom pom ties; black felt hat with iridescent green feather and red trim; 1930s. *Sandra Strater Collection.*

MARKS: "Germany//136.0."

Tyrolean Boy (Doll on left): 9in (23cm); all celluloid; Loden waistcoat with green trim; brown suede short pants with suspenders; red necktie; white shirt; green pointed hat with white feather; black cord trim around brim of hat; 1950s-1960s.

MARKS: "Eidelweiss Flower//Made in Austria" on one side of tag; "Seppel" on other side of tag. **SEE:** *Illustration 3, page 9.*

AZORES

The Portuguese Azores islands are located in the mid-Atlantic Ocean. They are an archipelago comprised of nine island groups. The population of about 300,000 lives mainly on farming and fishing. Ponta Delgada is the capital and chief port.

Azores Man: 7in (18cm); hard plastic head and body; molded hair; sleep eyes; vinyl hands; straw hat; lavender cotton print shirt; black cotton pants; 1960s-1970s.

MARKS: "S. MIGUEL - Azores" printed on cork base.

Azores Lady: 7.5in (19cm); pressed cloth painted face; cloth body over armature making movement possible; felt hands; blouse; red and white checked skirt; red and white checked scarf under bonnet of black cape; 1960s-1979.

MARKS: "BONECAS//RONOEL//AZORES" tag on skirt.

SEE: *Illustration 7, page 10.*

TINY BELGIUM - THE CROSSROADS OF EUROPEAN HISTORY

Belgium is a very densely populated, cosmopolitan country. There are three official languages: Flemish (Dutch), French, and German. The Flemish are the Dutch-speaking population, and they live in the Northern region near the Netherlands. Their customs are very similar to their northern neighbor. This region is called Flanders.

The people in the South are called Walloons and speak French. A few people in the eastern part of the country speak German.

Most of the other countries of Europe wear their provincial or ethnic costumes for festivals, weddings, etc. The people of Belgium love festivals, but these festivals cel-

ebrate historic battles, trade guilds, religious events, even cats. Often there are parades with costumes of army uniforms and from the medieval period.

The most unusual costume for a festival is the "Gilles" costume for men. It is a brightly-colored print, padded suit. The enormous hat is topped with huge ostrich feathers. The marchers toss oranges to the onlookers. This is to celebrate the victory over the Incas of Peru, and the oranges symbolize the gold taken by the Spanish soldiers.

The most celebrated "national" doll is the lace maker which many travelers bring home with them. Today the famous Belgian lace is no longer sewn by hand but made by machine.

The Unica Company is probably the most well known doll and toy maker in Belgian history. Founded in 1921 it made dolls in bisque, papier mâché, composition, hard plastic, and vinyl using the most advanced techniques of the period. Only a very few of their dolls could be considered provincial, regional or national dolls.

Lady with Milk Pails: 11.5in (29cm); painted mask face; mohair wig; cloth body; dark blue apron, green wool skirt; gray cape; brown, black, white wool blouse.
MARKS: "Brugeoise//5000/6"
SEE: *Illustration 8, page 11. Mary Tanner Collection.*

Unica
Liberated Belgium: 13in (33cm); glazed bisque head and arms; rather dark complexion like the other Unica dolls; large laughing mouth; cloth body; clothes are modern type of ethnic clothes; bright yellow blouse with pink trim; yellow, black, red striped skirt; black apron with pink ribbon trim; stones in head to immitate a rattle sound for children; 1945.

Immediately after World War II Unica began to manufacture dolls with whatever material was available. This doll was issued in honor of the liberation from German occupation, and for children who had been deprived of toys for years.
MARKS: "Liberated Belgium//Unica Patent// Courtray//Belgium" paper tag sewn to bottom of dress.
SEE: *Illustration 9, page 12.* A similar doll was made for Liberated Holland.

Emile Lang Belgian World War I Soldier (Doll on right): 14in (36cm); pressed mask face and head; oil-painted face and hair; inset tiny glass eyes; open mouth with painted teeth; sculptured ears on mask; papier mâché hands; cloth body and legs; felt khaki coat; black felt pants with red stripes; leather boots; tiny brass buttons; wooden rifle; ceramic canteen with real cork; cloth bag; circa 1917-1928.
MARKS: "E.L. Manufacture Francais//Jouettes Tissus//System Brevete//" on tag; "Belge" (handwritten on back of tag).
SEE: *Illustration 10, page 12.*
Emile Lang of France manufactured cloth dolls which were designed by Albert Guillaume and Jean Ray, well-known artists of the period. Lang was associated with the S.F.B.J. organization although he kept his own workshop.
Belgian Lacemaker (Doll in middle): 5.5in (14cm); all vinyl; gray thread wig; tiny glasses; velvet dress and bonnet trimmed with lace; in her

11

lap is a bobbin holder which helps keep the threads straight; 1968. This is the most popular "souvenir" doll in Belgium.

MARKS: "1968" on bottom of base.

Flandre (Flanders) Sailor (Doll on Left): 12.5in (32cm); all composition; painted eyes; jointed at shoulders and hips, molded painted white shoes; blue sailor suit; middy collar; striped undershirt; sailor hat with "Flandre" sewn on brim; 1930s. *Shirley Karaba Collection.*

MARKS: "FLANDRE" on sailor hat.

SEE: *Illustration 10, page 12.*

BULGARIA

Bulgaria is located north-east of the Balkan peninsula. It is a land that has been mostly agrarian. Despite the fact that about half of the population now live in cities, they are only one or two generations from farmers. Traditionally Bulgaria was a land of villages and regional craft centers. They have a tradition of rich folk art such as ceramics, wood carving, and weaving. They have attractive regional costumes, music, and dances, and like the rest of the world they are trying to hold on to their traditions. This can be seen through their dolls.

Dancing Bulgarian Girl (Doll on left): 7.5in (19cm); wood painted head; human hair wig; cloth over armature body; homespun material for clothes; white blouse with pattern stenciled on it; black skirt with embroidered ribbon trim at hem; long white petticoat with pattern stenciled around hem; red bolero and matching red apron with design stenciled on them; thread wound around armature for stockings; white oriental leather shoes with upturned toes; 1960s. *Lois Janner Collection.*
MARKS: "Made in Bulgaria" paper tag on bottom of stand.
Palm Sunday in Bulgaria Costumed Lady (Doll in middle): 15.5in (38cm); plaster-type composition head beautifully painted; very black hair and eyebrows; pink scarf tied in back of head; cloth body; clothes intricately decorated and embroidered; gold embroidered bolero with red trim; white cotton long-sleeved blouse; red pleated skirt embroidered with heavy yarn; striped apron; silk petticoat with hand-made lace which shows below the pleated skirt; wool stockings; oriental leather moccasins with black yarn ties; carries tamborine; silver-jeweled pin on red belt; 1930s.
MARKS: None on doll; "Palm Sunday in Bulgaria" hand written on tag.

Dancing Bulgarian Boy (Doll on right): 7.5in (19cm); wood painted head; white fur high hat; white cotton shirt with stenciled decorations; red belt; black twill knicker-type pants with stenciled decorations; white stockings with thread ties up to pants; white leather oriental shoes with upturned toes. *Lois Janner Collection.*
MARKS: "Made in Bulgaria" paper tag on bottom of stand.
SEE: *Illustration 12, page 13.*

The small dancing dolls are from the Sop region of western Bulgaria. They are performing the traditional *hora* dance.

This Bulgarian couple, *Shopes*, is from northwestern Bulgaria around the area of Sofia. The natives of each village have a particular embroidery on the hem, neck or arms of the *sukman*, a black overgarment which each wears. The trimming on the woman's white underskirt or *rieza* and her tied kerchief on her head also identifies her village. The leather peasant shoes are called *tzervoulie*.

Bulgarian Couple: 9.5in (24cm); European composition; cloth body; well-sculptured faces; 1930.

Woman (Doll on right): Human hair wig; silver earrings in ear; peach kerchief tied in an unusual fashion both in front and under her braid in back; white heavily embroidered blouse; black felt jumper with pink, blue, red wool stitching and white rickrack around hem; homespun cotton petticoat which shows embroidery around hem; maroon felt rectangular embroidered apron; hand crocheted trim; shoes missing, but they would look exactly like the man's.

Man (Doll on left): Matching costume; high fur hat; mustache painted on face; white embroidered homespun shirt; brown homespun pants; maroon belt with white yarn stitched design; white leather oriental shoes with upturned toes tied to ankle with black wool; carries long leather pouch with two pieces of wood which look like golf tees. This is a bagpipe-type musical instrument.

MARKS: "Kimport Dolls//Independence, Mo.// This doll//was made in//Bulgaria."

SEE: *Illustration 11, page 14.*

Czech Republic and Slovakia

Czechoslovakia consisted of three main divisions which at one time were independent areas and then were merged to form one country. They were Bohemia on the West, Moravia on the North, and Slovakia on the East. Recently Slovakia became an independent country, and Bohemia and Moravia became the Czech Republic.

The costumes in the West reflect the European designs. The costumes in the East are more Oriental.

In doing the research for this area, the authors found that the majority of the dolls made in these countries were made by the Lidova Tvorba Uh Brod Company. It is now represented in the United States by the Walmsley Company of Richmond, Virginia. One side of their older tags said, "The dolls were made in a Communist collective manufacturing Company." Tvorba means company.

Lidova Tvorba
Pizen Girl: 13in (33cm); hard plastic head; sticky vinyl legs and arms; vinyl body; white cotton

cap with lace trim and lace bow in back; white cotton blouse; red and black weskit tied in front; red skirt; white apron trimmed with lace, red embroidered ribbons hanging down front. 1960s; from the Bohemian area.

MARKS: "Ceskoslovensko" on box.

SEE: *Illustration 13, page 15. Louise Schnell Collection.*

Tatra Boy: 6.5in (17cm); all felt; felt eyes; embroidered mouth; all wool white embroidered pants; black wool embroidered vest; white cotton shirt with red felt cuffs; black "bowler-type" hat with red trim; 1960s.

Tatra Girl: 6in (15cm); black felt eyes; embroidered mouth; white felt blouse with black cuffs; white felt hat underneath black felt shawl; black felt pleated apron; white felt skirt; red felt bow in back; 1960s.

The dolls are from Slovakia.

MARKS: "Made in Czechoslovakia//hand made" on silver and blue Lidova Tvorba Uh Brod tag.

SEE: *Illustration 14, page 16. Louise Schnell Collection.*

Girl with Red Printed Headdress Folded over the Ears (Doll on left): 8in (20cm); European composition head; cloth body; painted face with unusually thick eye lashes; long white pleated sleeves with embroidered ribbon trim; white blouse with wide lace trim at neckline; green vest with white embroidered ribbon trim; rich tapestry short skirt with red flowers, green leaves, yellow background; green ribbon belt; high leather boots; attributed to the Hana area.

MARKS: None.

Borsice-venec Girl with Wreath Headdress (Doll on Right): 8in (20cm); hard plastic; cloth body; flowered wreath headdress; blue blouse with white collar; sleeves trimmed with pink ribbon; long red print multi-colored designs on skirt with lace trim; leather boots; from the area of Slovakia; 1950s-1960s.

MARKS: "Made in Czechoslovakia//Slovak Home Industry" on gold circle tag.

SEE: *Illustration 20, page 16.*

Neither of these two dolls seem to have been made by the Lidova Tvorba Company.

This is a delightful collection of the Piestany dolls from the Moravian section of Czechoslovakia from different years. Changes in the types of doll material, clothing material can be seen at a glance. They all have yellow and blue as their basic colors. The trims are all different. They were all made by the Lidova Tvorba Company in Czechoslovakia.

The man from this region wore an all white costume with blue looped trim and a low fur hat.

(Dolls Left to Right).

Soft Vinyl Head Doll: 11in (28cm); hard vinyl body; wigged; white blouse; blue ribbon vest; purchased by the owner's mother-in-law when she visited Czechoslovakia in the 1970s.

MARKS: "Lidova Tvorba Ud Brod" triangular tag. The rest of the dolls are not marked.

Shiny Hard Plastic Doll Head: 12in (31cm); soft vinyl body; molded head; blue print vest.

Dull Finish Celluloid Head: 12in (31cm); hard plastic body; molded head checked vest. It is difficult to determine the date of a celluloid doll of this period because many countries continued to

make the dolls even after they were declared a fire hazard.

All Hard Plastic Doll: 14in (36cm); wears a wig; blue print vest; 1950s.

All Hard Plastic Doll: 6in (15cm); no vest; 1950s.

SEE: *Illustration 17. Lois Jean Adam Collection.*

Czechoslovakian Dolls from Left to Right:

Zdiar Girl with White Babushka: 12.5in (32cm); she is from the area of Moravia.

Kyjov Girl (on box): 20in (51cm)

Small Kyjov Girl: 6in (15cm); soft vinyl.

Kyjov Girl: 15.5in (39cm)

Kyjov Boy: 12in (31cm); probably a bagpiper in the hills and mountains.

MARKS: None on dolls, but all were made by the Lidova Tvorba.

SEE: *Illustration 19, page 17. Lois Jean Adam Collection.*

16

Olsava Couple (Dolls on left): 4in (10cm); all vinyl.

Girl: blue dotted, pleated short skirt trimmed with lace; white blouse with large puffed sleeves; red kerchief hat; red belt; 1960s.

Boy: white pants; blue apron with embroidered ribbon at bottom of pants; embroidered red ribbon down the front of the apron, also used for a belt; white cotton shirt with blue ribbon trim; black fur-like hat with red ribbon; 1960s.

Bartered Bride (Dolls on right): 4in (10cm); all vinyl.

Girl: red skirt and vest over white blouse with lace trim; embroidered belt tied in front; black headdress with wide lace trim with big lace bow on back of hat; 1960s.

Boy: gold felt pants with looped trim; black vest with red looped trim; white shirt with blue embroidered ribbon at cuff line; 1960s.

MARKS: Lidova Tvora on boxes of both doll sets.

SEE: *Illustration 21, page 18. Louise Schnell Collection.*

Unknown Company

Moravian Girl: 8.75in (22cm); composition head and body; molded hair underneath mohair wig; white cotton blouse with black and red trim; black apron with ribbon of embroidered flowers; crocheted lace at edge; red print skirt with lace trim; garland of flowers in her hair; 1930s.

MARKS: "Higbee Company Cleveland, Ohio// Moravian Girl."

SEE: *Illustration 15, page 18. Dee Cermak Collection.*

Kojovijan Boy: 8.5in (22cm); white shirt; red embroidered bolero jacket with lace and embroidered ribbons hanging down front; red pants with looped black embroidery; flat black hat with white lace and red embroidery; green bow in front.

Kojovijan Girl: 8.5in (22cm); white blouse with large collar trimmed in black; large puffed sleeves with red and black trim; embroidered vest; blue pleated embroidered skirt with lace trim.

MARKS: "Panenky//Vceskoslovenskych Lidovych Krojich" on blue box.

SEE: *Illustration 16, page 19. Lois Jean Adam Collection.*

Old Czechoslavian Doll: 16in (41cm); molded celluloid head; painted face; heavy European cloth muslin body; red pom poms on chest attached to red felt; red, white, gray tapestry skirt; black cardboard boots; ribbon trim around hem; orange, red and white ribbons hanging down in front from waist; hand crocheted lace decorates collar sleeves; ties hanging down the front; beautiful hand embroidered bonnet with crocheted lace around edge near face; finely pleated sleeves. Doll attributed to area of Vicnov. However Olsava and Uhersky Brod-venec also had similar pleated sleeves.

MARKS: None.

SEE: *Illustration 22, page 19. Shirley Karaba Collection.*

Czechoslovakian Doll with Crown-Like Headpiece (Doll on left): 14.5in (37cm); heavy, beautifully painted hard plastic; sleep eyes; closed mouth; jointed at neck, shoulders, hips; red glitter thread hair; white blouse embroidery at neckline; red felt vest decorated with wide trim of silver sequins to waist; red belt heavily embroidered; red cotton pleated skirt with white lace and blue ribbon trim; black pleated skirt with lace trim and pink silk loop trim; green loop trim below pink trim; and handmade lace around the entire apron; white puffed sleeves have embroidered ribbon patch on each arm; sleeves pleated at cuffs; red felt matching crown with pink cardboard top; decorated with silver sequins; white felt shoes with red embroidery; Area of Zdiar-venec; 1950s.
MARKS: "LIDOVA TVORBA UH BROD" silver and pink scalloped tag.
Czechoslovakian Doll with Red Print Headdress (Doll on right): 12.5in (32cm); colorful papier mâché head with painted face; all cloth body; red cloth legs are part of body; cloth tied in knots at ears and ends hang down to waist; white muslin blouse with puffed lace trimmed sleeves; white and black print rectangular collar; blue satin vest trimmed with gold embroidered ribbon; red cotton pleated skirt; black apron with ribbon embroidery and hand crocheted lace at bottom edge; black leather shoes; attributed to the area of Kyjov; 1936-1940s.
MARKS: None.
SEE: *Illustration 18, page 20.*

DENMARK

Denmark is a small Scandinavian country full of beautiful little villages, blessed with good food and fresh air from the sea surrounding it. The people love the fun of the famous amusement park of Tivoli, the grandeur of Copenhagen, and the city of Odense, the home of Hans Christian Anderson.

It is a land of 500 islands and ferry connections, and yet it also connects to the European continent in Jutland and shares a continental sophistication with the rest of Europe. It is a happy place to live and a happy place to visit.

Copenhagen is on the island of Zealand. Funen is the second largest of Denmark's islands. Bornholm is 100 miles from Copenhagen.

Many of the cities seem to have their own costumes. Dolls purchased in Denmark from Amager, Mor, Dragor, Odense, Fano, Arhus and many others are usually clearly marked on the doll or box.

Copenhagen Mother and Baby: 6in (15cm) height of mother; mother dressed in red and black costume of Copenhagen; embroidered shawl around her shoulders; baby wrapped in blanket; 1957.
MARKS: "Copenhagen" on box.
SEE: *Illustration 27, page 21. Thelma Purvis Collection.*

LENCI

Copenhagen Girl: 17in (43cm) molded, pressed and painted felt face; cloth body; blonde mohair wig; white blouse with red embroidery; small, low green embroidered weskit; black skirt; striped apron; white felt pouch with colored decorations strapped around her waist; 1930s and into 1940s.

Lenci made a series of couples in International costumes. She used the #300 doll for the series. The costume is rather generic, but it identifies the boy and girl as Scandinavian.

MARKS: No label on doll but it is Lenci.
SEE: *Illustration 23, page 22.*

Girl from Mor: 8.5in (22cm); all hard plastic; sleep eyes; blonde thread wig; bonnet made of embroidered ribbons with pointed peak of black taffeta; pink ties on bonnet; pigtails; black skirt and top with black scarf heavily embroidered in red and green; white pleated apron with embroi-dered ribbon hanging down to the edge of pleated apron; 1966.

MARKS: "Diamond" with unreadable marks.
SEE: *Illustration 24, page 22.*

The Nissi are part of Christmas and everyday life in all of the Scandinavian countries. They are mischievous gremlins who live in the barnyards and attics of Danish Homes. If the family moves, the Nissi moves along with them. Nissi's name is a shortened version of St. Nicholas, but even in the middle of the summer when this picture was taken, they can be seen in the window of toy stores in Odense, Denmark. Pam is a musician, and she was entranced with the dancers, singers, and musicians in the window. She dashed into the store and soon came dancing out with the orchestra that can be seen in the picture.

Danish Nissi: 4in (10cm); wood ball head; mohair beards; cloth body on armature; heavy lead feet so they can stand; metal instruments; 1970s. (See *Illustration 159.*)

MARKS: None.

SEE: *Illustration 26, page 23.*

Arhus is an attractive town in Jutland which is the only part of Denmark attached to the European continent. The town has established an open air museum. The people have collected town houses from all parts of Denmark and brought them to this museum where they can be visited. The surroundings as you can see in the picture are beautiful.

Amager Island Girl (Doll on left): 7in (18cm); all hard plastic; sleep eyes; thread wig; blue dress with black and red trim; embroidered ribbons hang from the high waist; red crocheted lace around the hem; close-fitting cap on her head; 1977.

The dress is similar to an ancient bridal costume of Amager.

(Continued on page 24)

MARKS: "Amager" on box.

Doll from Dragor (Doll on right): 10in (25cm); papier mâché painted face and body; vinyl hands; thread hair; red pleated skirt with black jacket, hat and trim on skirt; the black scarf has beautiful red and green embroidery; the close-fitting black hat is unusual with its red trim. This doll is part of a whole series of Danish provincial dolls. Although they are small dolls, the workmanship is excellent; 1977.

MARKS: "Dragor" checked on a list of all the dolls that could be purchased in the line.

SEE: *Illustration 25, page 24.*

Boy in Danish Costume (Doll on left): 7in (18cm); hard plastic head and body; vinyl hands; black flannel coat and hat trimmed with yellow rickrack; black cotton pants; 1970s.

MARKS: "Denmark" on box.

Danish Soldier with Gun (Doll in middle): 6in (15cm); hard plastic with vinyl hands; sleep eyes; bearskin hat with ornament in front; gold epaulets; red felt coat with white ribbons across his chest; blue pants; gold buttons and gold ornament on chest; 1970s.

MARKS: None.

Peter Wessel (Doll on right): 7in (18cm); all hard plastic; sleep eyes; felt sailor suit with white collar; "Peter Wessel" on blue band on white sailor hat; 1950s.

Peter Wessel is a legendary folk hero from the Great Nordic War of 1715-1720. Norway and Denmark were one nation at the time, and they were at war with Sweden. After running away from home at 14, Peter became a sailor on a slave ship. He was a good sailor and the King promoted him to officer status. He rose through the ranks to be an Admiral. Norway and Denmark were poorer than Sweden and did not have the same equipment, but Peter won battles through trickery. Eventually Sweden lost the war, and today both Norway and Denmark hail him as their own hero. Later in 1720 he died in a duel in Hannover, Germany.

There have been many ships named the Peter Wessel, and even today the ferryboat between Copenhagen and Oslo is called the *Peter Wessel*.

MARKS: "Peter Wessel" on hat.

SEE: *Illustration 28, page 24.*

ENGLAND

England is a small island compared to many of the countries of Europe, with few "true" provincially costumed dolls. England is itself a province of Great Britain with its inhabitants idolizing the fashion of the King and Queen.

The dolls in this section trace the unusual customs of the people of the various sections of England. It also shows the older and unusual uniforms and symbols of a few Royal dolls.

Actually the majority of the British dolls the children played with parallel the dolls found in the United States at the same time. There are a few that are "distinctively" British.

THE ENGLISH CORN DOLLY AND BOBBIN DOLLS

The tradition of saving the last of the corn or grain each year as a sacrifice to the gods came from the legend of early civilizations such as Egypt, Babylon, Greece, India, China, Scandinavia, and Britain.

The legends in the British Isles vary from county to county, but these *Corn Dollies* are involved in many different rites to placate the Gods and ensure a good harvest the next year. Often there is a festival connected with this rite. Each of these festivals follow local traditions, and a study of them is interesting.

The present basic plaiting starts with only hollow stemmed straw, and wheat seems best for beginners although other grains are used as the dollmaker becomes more proficient. The name **Corn Dolly** is a generic name for all of the different types of these dolls.

At first all the figures were women as a symbol of fertility. However, now there are many different designs in different areas. The figure in *Illustration 29, page 26,* is one of the nine basic early models and is called the *Corn Maiden.* The American *Corn Husk* doll is another example of these dolls.

Another traditional doll in the British Isles is the *Bobbin Doll* made from cast off bobbins. These bobbins were used on the early modern cloth sewing machine which industrialized the trade. This started the flight of the people from living in small villages and

working the land to living in larger cities and working in the newly developing factories.

CHAD VALLEY

Grenadier Foot Guard: 18in (46cm); stiffened mask face; glass eyes; no ears; cloth body; velvet arms and legs; bearskin hat; red felt coat with white belt; black felt pants; circa 1935-1938.
MARKS: "Hygienic Toys//Made in England//by//Chad Valley Co. Ltd." (cloth tag sewn to the bottom of the feet.)
Small Grenadier Foot Guard: 7in (18cm); European hard plastic; same uniform, but he has lost his white belt; 1950s.
MARKS: None.
SEE: *Illustration 33, page 25.*

The picture in the background was taken at Windsor Castle.

Chad Valley made five types of *Foot Guards* that all use the same uniform. The *Grenadiers* have single spaced buttons on their tunic. The *Coldstream Guards* have pairs of buttons. The *Scots, Irish* and *Welsh Guards* have buttons in groups of three, four, and five respectively.

Corn Maiden (Doll on right): 9in (23cm) hollow straw body made pliable by soaking in hot water for 15 minutes; the straw was plaited into different forms.
MARKS: None.
Bobbin Doll (Doll on left): 8.5in (22cm); round carved wood head; wooden spindle on a base with a metal ring around the top; wooden plug for the neck fits into the hole in the top of the bobbin; arms are made of pipe cleaners curved around the bobbin with felt hands; dress material is typical English garden print cotton with lace trim; the face is painted on the wooden head; yarn hair; 1974.
MARKS: None
SEE: *Illustration 29, page 26.*

Visitors to London are often surprised to witness the royal treatment of people with pearl buttons sewn in patterns on their clothing receive. This custom started about 1900 by the "Flashboys", boys selling fruit from street carts. It was an advertising "gimmick" to attract customers. As the years past the decorations became more elaborate.

Eventually a competition was held to select the man and woman with the most flashy costume. They were crowned "Pearly King and Queen" and a festive ball was held to celebrate their victory.

As with English Royalty, this title became hereditary and passed to their children. Today there are few "Pearlies left", but they are the center of attention wherever they go.
Pearlie Lady: 13.5in (34cm); carved wood shoulderhead; painted face; cloth body and legs; leather arms; purple velvet dress covered with buttons in a fancy pattern; matching hat; 1910-1920.
MARKS: None.
SEE: *Illustration 30, page 26.*

Dean's Golliwog: 14in (36cm); all cloth; traditional black Gollywog; button eyes; painted face;

26

clothes also painted on cloth; yellow coat with red button sewn on; red pants; white "gaiters" black shoes. 1980s.

It is remarkable that no one has taken this doll out of its plastic container. Dean's says this is a fully washable toy by hand or machine. It can be spun dry.

The Golliwog has been part of British children's childhood for many years.

MARKS: "Dean's Traditional Golly//Dean's Childplay Toys//Rye Sussex, England.
SEE: *Illustration 38, page 27.*

Clothespin dolls have been very popular in England for many years. Both children and adults love to dress them. Local handmade ones are often found in the gift stores in museums and other points of interest where tourists visit, and where each of these dolls were purchased. The clothing follows many diverse themes, such as: historical figures, nursery rhymes, regional dolls and many others.

Clothespin dolls (Dolls from left to right): all approximately 4-4.5in (10-12cm); wood; and wigged.
Gypsy (a commom theme): black print dress; green apron with lace; red kerchief on head.
Lady of Fashion: lavender Liberty Print dress; matching hat; carries lavender basket filled with flowers.
School Teacher: black felt skirt; white and black striped shirt; traditional graduation hat; hickory stick.
Lady Taking a Stroll with her Black Poodle: gray, pink, blue, white Liberty Print dress trimmed with lace.

Mary, Mary Quite Contrary: blue dress with yellow flowers; white mob hat; carrying a wood stick garden tool.
Elegant Victorian Lady Out for a Stroll with her Umbrella: white, blue, lavender dress with pink lace trim; pink felt hat with huge flower on top.
MARKS: None.
SEE: *Illustration 32, page 27.*

For many years ships carried in their gift shops dolls with uniforms and inscribed hats displaying the ship name. In England these dolls were made by Norah Wellings, Alpha Farnell and other companies. The only way the owner can identify the manufacturer is by the tag on the doll. This doll does not have a tag.

Empress of England Sailor (Doll on left): 6.5in (17cm); hard plastic; suede-like blue sailor uniform; blue and white sailor hat; 1950s.
MARKS: "Empress of England" on band around hat.
Tower Guard of the Tower of London (Beefeater) (Doll in middle): 7in (19cm); all hard plastic; red and gold coat and leggings; stiff black hat; crown ornament on chest; carries a pike; 1950s.
MARKS: None.

English Bobby (Policeman) and his Police Dog (Doll on right): 7in (18cm); all hard plastic; dark blue suede police uniform and hat.
MARKS: None.
SEE: *Illustration 31, page 28.*

PEGGY NISBIT

Peggy Nisbit enjoyed sewing, making dolls, and loved British history. She sent Queen Elizabeth a doll for her Coronation. Much to Peggy's surprise, the Queen accepted her gift and recognized it officially. It was the beginning of an extraordinary woman's adventure into the doll world!

Today her dolls are known world wide, and she has been honored by the Queen for her contributions. Peggy Nisbit was one of the first to employ the handicapped. She started a cottage industry and parceled out the work each Monday and collected it again on Friday. Even in her assembly center she hired as many handicapped and blind persons as possible. She used the highest quality materials available including semi-precious stones.

She made dolls for the entire British Empire that were sold around the world. A book about European costumed dolls would not be complete without examples of her diverse products. Pictured are three women mon-

arch dolls. This grouping happened to be Nisbet's first experience with bisque dolls, and it was a very limited edition. It also shows the costumes of three very important eras in British history.

All of the dolls have the same general characteristics: 8.5in (22cm); bisque head, arms, legs; leather body; all three dolls were sculpted and dressed to match famous portraits.

Queen Elizabeth I (Doll on left): excellent portrait face; red hair; gold tapestry dress embroidered with semi-precious jewels; black cape; lace ruff around the neck.

Queen Elizabeth II (Doll in middle): modeled from the 25th anniversary portrait of her reign. The set included the gold throne seen in the picture.

Queen Victoria (Doll on right): modeled from the picture of her at an older age; the small table and red velvet cover came with the doll. The Bethnel Green Museum chose this doll to fill their historical collection of outstanding British doll artists and companies.

SEE: *Illustration 34.*

ALPHA FARNELL

Alpha Farnell is a remarkable British doll company famous for their *George VI, Coronation Doll* and the story involving its production.

When George the V died, his heir became King Edward VIII. The doll companies made preparations for the coronation which was to take place in months. Alpha Farnell was ready.

Suddenly Edward gave a radio address announcing his abdication. The world was shocked. The British Empire was dismayed. The Alpha Farnell Company, a maker of cloth dolls, was horrified. They had already started production of a coronation doll of *Edward VIII*. A few, very few, had already been sold.

these manufacturers, made rather small dolls 6-9in (15-23cm) documenting English history and symbolism. Over the years they issued hundreds of different dolls including a complete set of the Coronation of Elizabeth II in 1953.

Yeoman of the Guard (Doll on right): 9in (23cm); soft-sculpture face; cloth-over-armature body; painted face with gray whiskers; bright red, yellow, and black felt uniform; black hat with red trim; carries pike; another name is *Beefeater*; 1930s-1950s.

The uniform was designed during the Renaissance and has experienced few changes through the centuries.

MARKS: "Liberty//Made in England" on cloth tag sewn inside of coat.

John Bull (Doll on left): 9in (23cm); soft sculpture; "ample" felt body; top hat with gold buckle; white collar; blue coat; red vest; white pants; leather boots with red felt trim; 1930s.

John Bull is the British patriotic symbol much like Uncle Sam is the American patriotic symbol.

MARKS: "Liberty//Made in England" cloth tag; 1950s.

SEE: *Illustration 36, page 29.*

However, the story is that Alpha Farnell kept a "stiff upper lip" and stopped production; remodeled the face slightly slimmed down the full cheeks and chin, and started producing the *George VI, Coronation Doll.*

King Edward Coronation Doll (Doll on right): 13in (34cm); portrait; pressed felt painted mask face; ear made of single piece of felt, cotton stockinette arms and legs; cloth body; jointed at neck and shoulders; in full regalia of Coronation; 1937. This doll was part of the Pryor Collection.

MARKS: None. This is a very rare doll.

The Coronation regalia of George VI is almost identical.

George VI (Doll on left): same body description; full Highland dress with kilt, bearskin, sporran (pouch), and Order of Thistle; jacket trimmed with piping and gold braid; brass buttons, leather shoes with buckle; 1937-1939.

MARKS: "H.M.//THE KING//Made in England/ /by//J.K. Farnell & Co. Ltd//Acton, London//W3" on tag.

SEE: *Illustration 35, page 29.*

LIBERTY OF LONDON

Cloth dolls are very popular in England where some of the best cloth doll manufacturers are located. Liberty of London, one of

PENNY WOODEN DOLLS

The children of England loved the *Penny Wooden* dolls from Germany. They were inexpensive and fun to dress. Even Queen Victoria and her governess dressed many of these dolls now displayed in the London Museum. Many of the *Penny Woodens* were dressed in the costumes of the dancers of the day because Queen Victoria attended many ballets. She also dressed dolls in the fashions worn by her favorites at the court.

Old *Penny Wooden* dolls of this era are still available and some are in the collections of English doll lovers. There is a eager search for the old fortune telling dolls which the Victorian young English ladies made. Even Victoria used her doll to foretell her fortune. However dolls in good condition are hard to find as they were so well loved by their owners.

The doll in *Illustration 37* is an example of a 20th century *Penny Wooden* doll for collectors.

Souvenir Doll for Doll Exhibition (Doll on left): 6in (15cm); all wood; jointed at arms and legs; red blouse with white, black, green stripes on arms; green skirt with same color stripes at top and bottom; eyelet apron; 1963.

MARKS: "The Doll Exhibition//Oxford, May, 1963."

SEE:*Illustration 37, page 30.*

OLD COTTAGE DOLLS

One of the most famous companies producing costume dolls in England is the "Old Cottage Doll Company." These costume dolls are popular with both British and American collectors. In fact the American interest in these dolls has escalated their price in recent years. Unfortunately bad habitat conditions such as hot and cold temperature variations cause the heads to collapse.

Old Cottage Scottish Doll (Doll on right): 9in (23cm); special composition invented by the maker; cloth body; Royal Stuart kilt and scarf; black velvet jacket with lace cuffs; white shirt with lace ruff; Scottish hat with silver and gold ornament on both shoulder and hat; white fur sporron with silver handle; black leather shoes with white leather spats; purchased in the 1970s in the box in England. It is still in excellent condition.

MARKS: "Old//Cottage Doll Made in//England" one side of wrist tag. "Picture of an English Cottage" on other side of wrist tag.

SEE: *Illustration 37, page 30.*

ESTONIA

Estonia is one of the three small countries on the Baltic Sea that had been swallowed by the U.S.S.R. In spite of the fact that thousands of Estonians had been deported to eastern Russia and many Russian were resettled in Estonia, the brave people of Estonia managed to preserve their culture and national identity through songfests, writings, and traditional festivals where they wore their costumes. There are beautiful Estonian dolls both old and new for interested collectors.

Estonian Girl: 15in (38cm); European composition head and hands; cloth body and legs; mohair wig; beautifully painted face; heavily hand embroidered "Pill-box-type" hat; red jumper embroidered with black; top of skirt is also red; bottom of skirt is white with multicolored stripes with ribbon trim around hem; leather shoes; rayon stockings; well-made doll; 1930s.

MARKS: "Made in Estonia" printed on cloth tag sewn on inside hem of skirt.

SEE: *Illustration 39, page 31.*

FINLAND

The proud and patriotic Finnish people are finally independent after being a part of Sweden for seven centuries. Their language is related to the Hungarian and Estonian languages, but Swedish is a second language.

The Finnish traditional costume is gradually dying out, worn only on festive occasions. It consists of a full-sleeved blouse; long gathered skirt; a decorated apron and a square piece of cloth folded into a headpiece. Their decorative patterns are often geometric, like the costumes of Romania and other mideast European countries rather than the other Scandinavian decorations.

Finland Regions According to Statesman's Year Book 1990-1991
Provinces
1. Usimaa-Nyland
2. Turku-Pori-Bjorneborg
3. Shvenanmaa-Atland

4. Hame-Tavastehus
5. Kymi-Kymmene
6. Mikkeli-St. Michel
7. Pohjois-Karjala-Norra Karelen
8. Kuopio

9. Keski-Suomi-Mellersta Finland
10. Vaasa-Vasa
11. Voulu-Uleaborg
12. Lappi Lappland

Finnish Girl: 16in (41cm); European composition head, arms, hands, cloth body; two painted teeth; feathered eyebrows; beautiful blonde flax wig with braids; green felt jacket; red wool skirt; red embroidered overvest; white cotton apron with hemstitching and hand-crocheted decorations; black shoes; 1930s-1950s.

Turku is an industrial city on the west coast of Finland dotted with forests and lakes. It hosts a musical festival each year.

MARKS: "Marta//Turku ABO" on circular tag sewn on apron.

SEE: *Illustration 42, see page 32. Ester Borgis Collection.*

Finnish Boy (Doll on left): 5.5in (14cm); well-made European hard plastic; non-jointed; painted face and hair; blue felt tam-like hat; white shirt; red felt vest with painted white buttons; glue felt short pants with white stitching for decoration; painted red stockings; painted black shoes; 1970s.

Finnish Girl (Doll on right): 5.5in (14cm); well-made European hard plastic; non-jointed; brown mohair wig with red felt band; white blouse; fringed, white, red, and green print scarf; red, black, green, yellow, white, striped short skirt; white apron with red trim; painted red socks; painted black shoes; 1970s.

MARKS: "Turun Martta-Nukketeollisuus//Made in Finland" on lid of plastic container.

SEE: *Illustration 41, page 32.*

Finnish Eskimo Baby: Semi-hard vinyl; dressed in white fur with red and yellow trim; leather shoes; purchased at the Arctic Circle in Finland in 1970. Price at that time was $75.

MARKS: "Finnish Design by Noitarumpu Rovaniemi//Finland" label on left shoe.

SEE: *Illustration 40, page 33. Thelma Purvis Collection.*

The Forever Fashionable Dolls of France

For many years France has been the world capital of new fashion. This love of clothing and quality costumes is reflected in French provincial doll costumes.

The costumes of the provinces within France are very different. Yet all of the costumes have a sense of high style. The variety of provincial dresses seems endless because each individual city or village has variations of the basic regional costume. The headdresses throughout France are very elaborate and unique, often identifying the province or city.

The quality of the French dolls dressed in folk costumes is generally high. The French have taken the typical "tourist doll" and created some of the most beautiful art dolls. In keeping with French "high fashion" the costumes of these dolls are made from fine fabrics such as velvet, satin, brocade with elaborate lace and braid.

Bisque, celluloid, papier mâché, and hard plastic dolls have been used in this century, and now there are lovely vinyl dolls being dressed in the traditional ways.

In Southern France the art of the Santon doll is especially popular. These dolls are displayed at the Christmas markets and chosen by children as additions to the Christmas creche scene. These figures are more than traditional Creche figures. They serve as representations of the people of the surrounding country side.

In the past characters such as the baker, the woman with a baby in a cradle on her head, or the mayor were placed in the Nativity scene along with the Christ Child. Today modern workers are added, and they too join the Wise Men hurrying down from the hills

to see the Baby in the manager (see *Illustration 66, page 48.*)

The artisans of Southern France sculpt, mold, and paint these Santons (Little Saints) by hand. Until recently these figures were made of clay, dried in the sun and painted. Now they are fired if they are to be shipped. Both styles are popular in France.

Some of the figures are as small as one half of an inch (1.2cm). Some of the most popular figures are only three inches (7.6cm) but all are as lifelike as the skill of the "santonniers" can make them. These figures are passed down from one generation to another.

Provinces of France
1. Normandy - North across from England.
2. Brittany - A peninsula extending into the Atlantic.
3. Anjou - South of Brittany on the coast.
4. Poitou - South of Anjou on the coast.
5. Aquitaine - South section of France.
6. Gascony - Bordering the Pyrenees Mountains.
7. Picardy - North bordering Belgium.
8. Ile de France - Region around Paris and Versailles
9. Champagne - North to the east of Picardy.

10. Burgundy - South of Champagne (Central France).
11. Languedoc - South along Mediterranean Coast.
12. Lorraine - East bordering Germany.
13. Alsace - East bordering Germany.
14. Provence - Southeast on Mediterranean Sea.
15. Corsica - An island in the Mediterranean Sea.

Normandie Doll: 7in (18cm) from top of hat to feet; celluloid; jointed arms and legs; lace and satin hat tied with ribbons; lace shawl; black velvet skirt with embroidered braid edged wtih gold at the botton of skirt; gold chain around her neck with cross; mohair hair; ankle length bloomers; painted socks and shoes.
MARKS: "Ma Normandie Poupeé" tag on arm; "Made in France" on back of tag.
SEE: *Illustration 48, page 34. Nancy Gallaher Collection.*

LE MINOR FRANCE

Baby Babig-Koant: 10in (25cm) celluloid baby; bent legs; embroidered organdy dress and embroidered ribbon trim in gold; same material for apron and dress; gold chain with pendant; satin hat embroidered with gold and beads; hat tied under chin in large bow; puffed sleeves with same braid as apron and dress.

In 1951 the Associated Press showed a picture of this doll. General Dwight Eisenhower received the doll from the grateful people of Brittany and presented it to the National Museum in Washington D.C.
MARKS: "Je Suis un//Bebe Bretan//on m'appelle//Babig-Koant" one side of tag. "Le Minor" other side of tag.
SEE: *Illustration 45, page 34. Sandra Strater Collection.*
For more information about Madame Le Minor, see page 36.

French Lisieux Woman Candy Container (Doll on left): 6.75in (17cm); molded plaster, painted head; stuffed cloth upper torso mounted on cardboard tube; plaster forearms with clasped hands; plaster lower legs with sabots; bottom of tube is mounted on legs to complete candy container; kerchief on head; black, red, white shawl; red skirt; plaid apron; 1926.
MARKS: None on doll; "Lisieux France//Sunday July 4, 1926", handwritten on tape on doll.
SEE: *Illustration 47, page 35.*
Pont-Aven Brittany Girl (Doll on right): 11in (28cm); composition head; five piece slender composition body; stationary glass eyes; molded, painted composition shoes; black silk dress with bold metallic braid; moire apron; pleated white collar edged in lace; starched lace provincial headdress.
MARKS: "S.F.B.J.//PARIS" on back of head.
SEE: *Illustration 47, page 35. Shirley Karaba Collection.*

Girl from Benodeten: 7in (18cm); all-celluloid; headdress consists of a high lace coif under which the hair is tightly help up by a small bonnet; there are elaborate lace wings on each side; red velvet dress with flowered braid; 1950s.
MARKS: "My name is Marine. I am from Benodeten in Brittany" on dress label.
SEE: *Illustration 46, page 35. Pat Parton Collection.*

BRITTANY DOLLS

Madame Le Minor was a native of the provence of Brittany and one of the best known designers of Brittany dolls. She purchased dolls of different materials including celluloid, papier mâché, composition, and hard plastic. She designed spectacular outfits, and also made costumes from other provinces for each type of doll. Her workshop was started in the 1930s.

Madame Le Minor purchased celluloid dolls from Peticolin and Société Nobel Francaise. Peticolin's mark is the head of an eagle with France printed under it. The trademark of SNF is the initials SNF inside a diamond.

Dolls from Quimper: 14in (36cm); bisque socket head; cloth body; celluloid hands; reddish mohair wig; painted eyes and eyelashes; arms, legs sewn on to the body; red felt dress with opulent embroidered ribbon near bottom of dress; white satin apron with gray heavily embroidered trim with gold edges; hat is unique to region with its cut-off triangular style overlaid with lace; heavily embroidered gold ribbons over hat and fastened with a bow just above the waist; early 1930s.
MARKS: "Je M'Appelle//Corentine//Mon pays es// Quimper//En Bretagne" on wrist tag.
SEE: *Illustration 43, page 36.*

SOCIÉTÉ NOBEL FRANCAISE
Girl from Quiberon, Brittany: 11in (28cm); late all-celluloid; ornate black velvet dress with gold apron. Embroidered braid encircles her skirt and sleeves. Her bodice is trimmed with sequins and gold trim; 1970s.
MARKS: "SNF (within a diamond)" on back of doll; "Designed by Blance Jantier of Paris" label on dress.
SEE: *Illustration 44, page 36.*

HISTORICAL DOLLS
Many of the countries of Europe are not only trying to preserve their costumes, but they are trying to preserve history through their dolls. Their musuems are full of wonderful dolls (antique to modern) where children and people of all ages can go to learn about history. This book would not be complete without some of the historical French figures.
Marie Antoinette (Doll on left): 7in (18cm); all celluloid; white powdered hair in the fashion of

the period; light blue dress trimmed with white ruffles; gold trim; three black velvet bows down the front of the dress; fan with feathers in right hand; 1961.

King Louis XVI (Doll on right): 8in (22cm); all celluloid; white powdered hair of the period; white velvet coat and knicker-type pants trimmed in gold braid; white pom poms on each side of the pants; black shoes with gold buckles; lace jabot; gold walking stick; black tricorn hat trimmed in gold; 1961.

MARKS: "Les Poupees//de//Marly//Marie Elizabeth Perret//258 Rue de Rivoli//Paris" label on stand.

SEE: *Illustration 50, page 37. Louise Schnell Collection.*

Boy and Girl Dressed in Costumes of the Nobility of the late 1700s: 17.5in (43cm) both dolls; smooth felt faces; cloth bodies; unusual inset in each arm to hold composition hands; no ears; jointed at neck, shoulders, hips; beautiful painted face; very wide eyebrows; white mohair wigs (imitating powdered wigs of period); brown eyes with white semicircle under each pupil; white dot on left side of eye; two white dots imitating teeth on lower lip; cloth body.

Girl (Doll on left): pink silk blouse; lace scarf with dark pink trim; felt skirt with same trim; lace apron with same trim; yellow hat with matching darker pink trim and flowers; white stockings; leather shoes that button at the side.

Boy (Doll on right): dark blue velvet suit of the late 1700s trimmed with dark blue rickrack; lace at sleeves; lace jabot at neckline; dark blue ribbon tied at bottom of pants; gold brocade long vest with pearl buttons; beige stockings; leather shoes with big silver buckles; both dolls were all original; 1920s

The building in the background is the Chateau Chambord in the Loire Valley.

MARKS: "RAYNAL" on the girl's necklace and soles of her shoes. "Raynal" on the soles of the boy's shoes.

SEE: *Illustration 51, page 37.*

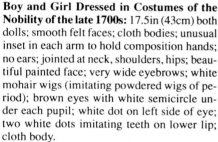

Raynal usually made dolls with cloth heads. However, a few were made with celluloid heads. The hands were usually made of cloth or celluloid, but these hands were different from other Raynal hands. They had a ball attached to the composition hand that was inserted inside a pouch sewn into the arm.

Justine of St. Lo: 9in (23cm); all vinyl; dressed in red skirt with a yellow apron; trimmed with braid; her high headdress is made of net and fluted lace.

Normandy is in the north of France adjoining Brittany.

MARKS: "Peticolin" on doll; "I am Justine of St. Lo" on tag.

SEE: *Illustration 49, page 38. Louise Schnell Collection.*

Girl from Alsace-Lorraine: 14.5in (37cm); bisque character face; slender papier mâché body; open/closed mouth with inset teeth; painted eyes; large bow-like headdress; red insignia in middle; lace ruff around neck; light organdy white blouse; yellow tapestry with black design across chest (called a plastron); dark red belt and stripes on side of red dress; black silk apron; blue garters on bloomers; black shoes; red band at hem; 1915-1924.

The band at the hem indicates the religion. Red is for Catholic; white is for Protestant; mauve is for Jewish.

MARKS: "No oll Ale © 2//Limoges".

SEE: *Illustration 55, page 38. Sandra Strater Collection.*

(Back Row from left to right).

Girl from Gascogne: 7in (18cm); vinyl; straw bonnet tied with red ribbon on right side; red taffeta dress; white embroidered apron; white trim to make it look like a vest on chest; gold cross. 1970s.

MARKS: "Gascogne" on underskirt.

Member of the Nobility: 6in (15cm); all-celluloid; wig with top knot; blue brocade dress; red velvet cape in the same blue brocade; gold crown; gold stars on bodice of dress; 1965.

This doll was purchased at a shop called Hermes-Paris in France.

MARKS: None on doll.

SEE: *Illustration 54, age 39.*

Girl from Champagne: 7in (18cm); celluloid; brown hair orange dress; green apron trimmed with gold and lace; burgundy ribbon around bottom of skirt; square starched lace bonnet; (see *Illustration 68.*); for more information; 1960s.

MARKS: "Champenoise" on circular tag.

(Front Row from left to right).

Girl from Boulogne: 3.5in (9cm); all-vinyl; fully jointed; black and blue brocade apron; black silk shirt trimmed with gold rickrack; fluted (pleated) stand-up starched headpiece; purchased at Printemps Department Store in Paris; 1960s.

MARKS: "C'est une//creation//Phillippe" on tag; shield of Toulouse on top of package.

SEE: *Illustration 54, page 39.*

Boulogne is in the province of Champagne in Northern France on the border of Belgium. Boulogne is on the Atlantic Ocean. Other cities in the province are Reims, Arras, Amiens (which is the capital of Picardy).

Girl from Toulouse: 3.5in (9cm); hard-vinyl; very detailed for such a small doll; purple skirt; black apron with large red flowers and other embroidery; straw bonnet under chin; 1960s.

Toulouse is a major town in the Midi-Pyrenees province. It is only about a two hour drive from Spain, and Toulouse is a town with a Spanish-flavor. Other towns in the province are Bordeaux, Lourdes, Carcassone (see *Illustration 62, page 42*). It is also on the border of Andorra.

MARKS: "C'est une//Creation//Phillipe" top of plastic container.

SEE: *Illustration 54, page 39. Louise Schnell Creation.*

Pas de Calais Girl: 12in (31cm); painted bisque head; glass sleep eyes; feather eyebrows; eyelashes under eyes; open mouth with four teeth; red mohair wig; wooden body jointed at neck, shoulders, elbows, wrists, hips, knees; blue silk blouse and matching pleated apron; dark red skirt; red and white print shawl with black ribbon trim below shoulders; "halo effect" pleated headdress trimmed with lace; gold bead "lappets" hanging down from back of each side of bonnet; dress is very unusual because it has a high waist. Calais is directly across the English Channel from the Kent Coast.

MARKS: "SFBJ//PARIS//3" engraved on back of neck.

SEE: *Illustration 56, page 39.*

S.F.B.J. made a series of these provincial dolls. The dolls are excellent, but the clothes are very different from the ones made by other companies.

Alsace-Lorraine Pedlar Woman (Doll on left): 14in (36cm); needle-sculptured, painted stockinette face; gray mohair wig; flesh-colored jersey stuffed body over wire armature; wooden shoes; black Alsace-Lorraine headdress; blue and brown crocheted shawl with white trim; white blouse; red felt skirt with black trim; black petticoat and bloomers; April 1972.

Her basket is filled with miscellaneous tools, charms, kitchenware, fruit and other assorted articles.

MARKS: "Original Ravca//Paris-New York" one side of tag; "Frances Diecks Ravca//April-1972" on other side of tag.

Brittany Fisherman (Doll on right): 10in (25cm) needle-sculptured stockinette painted face; padded wire stockinette body and limbs; blue cotton suit; white and blue striped undershirt; red tie; wooden shoes; 1924-1939.

MARKS: "Original//Pecheur" on paper tag; "B. Ravca" signature; "Made in France" tag sewn in back of shirt.

SEE: *Illustration 52, page 40. Shirley Karaba Collection.*

Thumette of Pont-l'Abbe: 13in (33cm); painted bisque jointed head; cloth body; black velvet skirt with three rows of gold trim near bottom of skirt; black velvet bodice heavily embroidered with orange thread; very high stiff white lace headdress with lace ties under the chin.

This doll is not marked with the LeMinor label. The company on the gold tag also on a cloth strip on her skirt is "Fabrication Bretonne Broderie Main Les Poupees."

MARKS: "Je m'appelle THUMETTE// mon pays est PONT-L'ABBE en Bretagne" on gold wrist tag.

SEE: *Illustration 53, page 40.*

Poupees Venus (from Arles): 16in (41cm); felt head; cloth body; celluloid hands; brown real hair wig; long thin eyebrows; two-tone lips with two small teeth painted on lower lip; tight curls around bottom of hair; straight bangs; eye shadow and beautiful painted eyes; gold cross around neck; dressed in blue dress; black apron with lace; white chiffon shawl over shoulders; headress is black taffeta with gold crown; white slip and teddy; black shoes late 1920s; all original; early 1930s.

This was the trade name of Adrien Carvaillo who sometimes distributed dolls through Bon Marche, a Paris store.

MARKS: "POUPEES//VENUS//PARIS//MADE IN FRANCE" on tag sewn on apron; "AU BON MARCHE PARIS//JOUETS//9F" tag on wrist.
SEE: *Illustration 58, page 41.*
This doll is often mistaken for the Raynal Doll. It is very similar.

The city of Lourdes in southwest France has a shrine that has been a major center for pilgrimages for people of Catholic faith ever since the 14-year-old Bernadette Soubirous had her vision of the Virgin Mary. This shrine particularly attracts the sick and infirmed. They come from all over the world with their families and friends to the famous grotto where she had her vision. The picture in the background shows the nuns helping the people in wheel chairs and the others who have gathered to pray.

Bernadette Doll: 12in (31cm); celluloid painted mask face and molded hands; mohair wig; cloth body; dressed in Nun's habit; wooden, molded shoes; 1930s.
MARKS: None.
SEE: *Illustration 59, page 41. Sandra Strater Collection.*

Lanternier Provincial Girl: 16.5in (42cm); bisque head; stationary blue glass eyes; fully jointed composition body; open/closed mouth with 6 molded teeth; cream body suit; tan wool vest; beige dress with orange trim; white stockings and black shoes; black beaded hat with gray draped veil hanging down the back; 1917-1921.
MARKS: "Je Masson//Lorraine No. D//A.L. & Cie//Limoges."
SEE: *Illustration 57, page 42. Shirley Karaba Collection.*

The Lanternier Company was known to have made provincial dolls of Bourg, Arles, Alsace. This doll has many characteristics of the Bourg-de Batz dolls of Brittany, but it is quite different from the interpretation of the same costume by Madam Le Minor.

This doll was probably dressed by Baroness de Laumont who around 1920 dressed novelty dolls in the peasant costumes of the French Provinces using Laternier bisque heads.

The Unis Company was started in France right after World War I. It was a type of trade association well-known for its French provincial dolls. This little boy was purchased by Polly in a small antique doll store in the fully restored fortress of Carcassone in southern France.
Brittany or Normandy Boy: 13.5in (34cm); papier mâché head; jointed composition body; blue glass eyes; bright red hair with tiny braid encircling head; all black suit and jacket; gold trim and gold buttons; 1920s.

The fortress can be seen in the background.
MARKS: "Unis//France" in oval, "71" on body.
SEE: *Illustration 64, page 42.*

Girl from Lyon: 10in (25cm); European hard plastic; wears blue satin dress with flowered braid; white lace apron; 1970s.

The city of Lyon is on the Rhone River west of the Alps and Switzerland.

MARKS: "Poupees Folklorique//Maguy//Lyon."

SEE: *Illustration 62, page 43.*

Doll from Cannes (Doll on left): 9in (23cm); all vinyl; straw bonnet over scarf; blue and white striped skirt which is typical of the region; she carries a basket of flowers. She is from the Province of Provence.

MARKS: "SNF Eagle Head in Diamond."

Girl from Nice (Doll on right): 8in (20cm); all-vinyl; straw bonnet over scarf; wears a red and white blouse; black embroidered apron; carries a basket of flowers.

Nice is a beautiful city in Provence on the Mediterranean Sea. The colorful costume is often still seen in the tourist area. 1970s.

MARKS: None.

SEE: *Illustration 63, page 43. Louise Schnell Collection.*

These are the typical dolls from Provence, especially the city of Nice. Many who have this costume also have a basket of flowers and are called the *Flower Sellers.* However, there are other costumes, especially ones using print materials.

Provence Girl (Doll on left): 14in (36cm); cloth body; silk face; blue eyes with real lashes; celluloid hands; red floss wig and upper eyelashes; white taffeta dress with red stripes; black lace trim around bottom of skirt; weskit with black ties,

scarf with black trim; felt apron; red and white striped skirt with black band near the bottom; early 1930s.

This doll has many Raynal characteristics.

MARKS: None.

SEE: *Illustration 69, page 44. Sandra Strater Collection.*

Sardane Dancers: 8in (20cm); all cloth.

The Eastern Pyrnees Region in both Spain and France is Catalon country. The life and customs on both sides of the border are basically the same. This is a land of trails across beautiful mountains and gorgeous valleys, and walking through the countryside is a way of life (see *Illustration 216* in the Spanish section of this book).

Since about 1920 both the Spanish and the French have revived their folk costumes of the past, and because they love to dance, they have folk dance festivals which you can see in *Illustration 61, page 45.* The dance they love is called the Sardane.

These dolls were made in 1964 in a camp for children in the Pyrnees mountains on the French side of the border. They show the costume of the dance and the position in which it is danced.

white silk blouse; straw hat with painted flowers around the brim.

This doll is very different from the Raynal doll.

MARKS: None.

Raynal Provence Girl (Doll in middle): 24in (61cm); cloth body; silk face; celluloid hands; side-glancing eyes with gray paint around the pupil; brown eyes with white highlight in each eye; excellent color; same material and costume as smaller doll; black silk apron; print scarf around neck; gold cross; straw embroidered hat; carries basket of roses; early 1930s.

MARKS: None.

Provence Girl (Doll on right): 14in (36cm); all felt; instead of hat the doll has two tri-color ribbons, one on each side of mohair wig; cloth body and hands; excellent color; brown side-glancing eyes; gray around eyeball; white highlights in each eye; legs seamed at back only; flower print

The dolls are truly folk art made by the children in the camp where our son and brother, Wally Judd, was an A.F.S. exchange student. He took the picture and brought home the dolls. They have no faces because the emphasis is on the clothes and the dance.

However, in this borderland, different valleys have variations of the costumes as can be seen in the picture. The costume on these dolls is very close to those of the Spanish. There are commercial dolls with similar costumes (see *Illustration 216.*)

MARKS: None.
SEE: *Illustration 161, page 140.*

Folk Dancing: Along with the dolls, folk dancing festivals and contests are popular ways of preserving the culture of the villages, cities, and countries. There are countless festivals throughout Europe as each ethnic group enjoys keeping its traditions.

This is a picture of a folk dancing contest. A judge can be seen in the center of the picture scoring the dancers. This festival took place in 1963 in the Catalon region in the Pyrenees which spans two countries, France and Spain.

The villages in the deep valleys of the Pyrenees in both countries have developed their

own costumes, but they all dance the "Sardane". The costumes on the dolls in *Illustration 61, page 45* can be seen on the dancers on the left center of the picture.

Another folk dancing scene can be seen in *Illustration 230, page 145* in Malmo, Sweden.

Dancing dolls can be seen throughout this book.

CHAMPENOISE (Champagne Dolls)

Champenoise (Doll on left): 9in (23cm); all-celluloid; distinctive headpiece is the same as the 8in (20cm) doll; this headpiece also has three rows of lace with two tiny pieces of red ribbon on either side of headpiece; reddish, brown marcelled wig; excellent details on painted face; red satin dress lined with stiff net; yellow satin apron trimmed with lace at hem; lace shawl; molded painted high-high-heeled shoes; 1939-1960+.

MARKS: "FRANCE//SNF (IN DIAMOND)" on back of body; "La Poupee Artistique" printed on box.

The SNF (in a diamond) was the mark of the Société Novel Francais. These dolls were used for regional costuming by Les Fetiches Nicois in Nice. They were also used by Martel Company for regional dolls. SNF registered their trademark in 1939 and again in 1960.

Champenoise (Doll on right): all-celluloid; distinctive headpiece has three rows of lace, squared off on the top, with two tiny pieces of black ribbon on either side of the top row of lace; reddish, brown mohair wig; excellent details on the painted face that is typical of celluloid dolls; blue taffeta dress with net shawl trimmed with lace; pink taffeta apron trimmed with lace; plastic cross on tiny chain; late 1920s.

MARKS: "(Head of Eagle)//France" on body and on tag. "Champenoise//(Head of Eagle) Jouet de France//Champenoise" on box.

This is the sign of the Petitcolon Company of France. They made celluloid dolls of various sizes and prices. Some of the dolls, even the small ones, used excellent fabrics for their clothes. Other dolls from the same company had costumes of cheaper material and were less expensive. The company was started in 1902 and lasted until the late 1920s. One of their customers was Madame Le Minor, a major doll artist of the period. Celluloid, a first step towards discovery of hard plastic material, was perfected during World War II. Since celluloid was a fire hazard, many companies of the world banned it after the war and started using vinyl. France continued celluloid production longer than most other countries.

SEE: *Illustration 68, page 45.*

SANTONS

During the Christmas season the people of Provence in Southern France go out into the hills and bring back rocks, small branches, and moss to build the setting for their "Cribs" which are featured in houses and churches during the Christmas season.

Terra Cotta figures, known as "Santons" (little Saints) have been made by families, artisans, and professional artists for many, many years. The old ones are carefully preserved from generation to generation. If the family does not make them, they will go to the markets and choose the new additions for the year much like we choose our new Christmas tree ornaments.

The Santons are representatives of the people of Provence. They join with the Wise Men on their journey to see the Christ Child. The farmers, the butcher, the baker, the candlestick maker, the women with cradles on their heads, and the new ones such as the painter who brings his painting as a gift to the Baby (see *Illustration 67, page 47.*) are some of the many figures. The old ones are treasured; the new ones admired each year. The Santons are so intriguing that they have been brought back by travelers to their homes in many lands.

These Santons range in size from about 1in (3cm) to life-size figures. Some are primitive. Others are works of art.

Man with Bed Warmer and Candle (Doll on left): 11.5in (29cm); baked clay; sculptured face of old man; blue pants; white and blue checked shirt; bright red scarf and sash.

This is an old man on his way to bed with a copper bed warmer and a small candle. There are Santons for many occasions; 1970s.

In the past most of the doll artists did not sign their work. Today some of them do.

MARKS: "S. Jouglas" engraved on bottom of base.

Mother Carrying a Cradle on Her Head (Doll on right): 11.5in (29cm); baked clay; red and white print dress is quilted for warmth; flocked collar which is typical of the region area; white bonnet; red apron; 1970s.

This mother carries her child in a cradle on her head down the long walk to visit the manger.

MARKS: None.

SEE: *Illustration 65, page 47.*

The Santon Painter: 10in (28cm); all-terra cotta; man with gray hair and whiskers; felt black hat; white painter's smock with dabs of paint on it; blue print scarf; holding pallette and brush; his painting is of a scene in Paris; 1991.
MARKS: "Atelier Gasquet."
SEE: *Illustration 67, page 47.*

Journey of the Santons: 3in (8cm); all of these tiny people are winding their way down the hills of Provence to pay homage to the Christ child in the manger at the bottom of the picture. This scene has hung in a home in Scotia, New York, for many years. The small figures had been collected over a long period of time, and finally put in this display.

There are many ways to collect and display Santons. One of the most beautiful scenes is in the National Musée of Monaco where the figures are almost life size.
MARKS: Most Santons of this small size are not signed.
SEE: *Illustration 66, page 48. Carlton Brown Collection.*

Germany

This is an excellent time to research the costumes of the various areas of Germany. The country is united, and eager to revive many of the customs of yesteryear. Travelers in the last year or two see the return of old customs, and for the first time in many years, museums and research are open to all.

However, it is also a time of change. Provinces have consolidated, and changed names. It will take a while to get used to the "New Germany", and the identification of costumes will not be done exactly as they are done in the other sections of this book.

One of the problems is that the dolls and costumes are different even within the individual cities, towns, and hamlets of the same province. The second problem is that there are not only provincial costumes, but there are also regional costumes (example the Black Forest region). The third problem is a literary legacy of costuming as left to us by the Brothers Grimm and other keepers of the folktales.

German dolls, old and new, are among the favorites of doll collectors. The authors will show you examples of many of these areas, but there are many, many more. After all, Germany was the doll capital of the world for a long time, and in the hearts of Germans they still are.

Provinces of Germany Since October, 1990
1. Bayern (Bavaria).
2. Baden-Württemberg Saarland.
3. Rhineland-Palatinate.
4. Hessen (Hesse).
5. Nordrhein Westfalen. (North Rhine-Westphalia).
6. Neidersachsen. Lower Saxony.
7. Schleswig-Holstein
8. Thüringen
9. Brandenburg (Berlin)
10. Sachsen (Saxony) and Thuringia.
11. Sachsen-Anhalt
12. Mecklenburg-Vonpommern
13. Hamberg and the Northern Islands
14. Baltic Coast and Lubeck.
15. Franconia.

Another Way to Look At the Old Costumes of Germany by Regions
1. Munich-the city founded by a monk (Monk of Munchen).
2. Bavarian Alps including such cities as Garmisch, Oberammergau. Berchtesgaden.
3. The Bodensee: Lake Constance region; Alpine area bordering Switzerland and Austria.
4. The Bavarian Forest and Passau.
5. The Black Forest region including Freiburg.
6. The Romantic Road: Wurzburg, Rothenburg-ob-der-Tauber. This region has nothing to do with romance. It was the road used by the Romans as they headed north.

Land of the Brothers Grimm
1. The Fairy-tale Road from Frankfurt to Bremen; the land of the Brothers Grimm.

ROTHENBURG-OB-DER-TAUBER

The journey through Germany includes a stop on the Romantic Road in the famed walled city of Rothenburg. Most of the cars are parked outside the wall, and as first-time visitors round a corner, this wondrous view greets them. For the doll lover and collector, this is a magical city.

Rothenburg houses a famous doll museum with beautiful creche scenes from all around the world. The best of the German antique dolls can be seen upstairs if you can get past the lovely, small gift shop. The magic of the *Christkind* (doll on left) points the way.

The *Rattenfanger* (doll on right) also known as the *Pied Piper of Hameln* (Hamlin) will pipe you down the hill to another magical treat. Here is the world-famous Christmas store of Käthe Wohlsahrt. There you can experience Christmas year round. Try to save time for a walk around the wall of this romantic town.

Christkind (The Christmas Angel) (Doll on left): 6in (15cm); all vinyl; jointed at shoulders only; well-painted face; white mohair wig; dressed in lace dress with bold trim; gold hairband with gold star; shiny gold belt and angel wings; 1992. Over the years there have been many versions of this doll made both by companies and by doll artists.

The German children of some provinces leave the window open on Christmas Eve for the An-

gel. She slides down a shiny rope bearing gifts from the Christ Child.

MARKS: "Trachtenpuppen Wiegand; Stoll's Trachtenpuppen zum Sammeln Handarbeit." seal on box.

Rattenganger (Doll on right): 5in (13cm): hard plastic head; vinyl hands; cloth body; painted face; sleep eyes; felt suit in blue, red, green and yellow; purple cape; red and green cap with large feather. He carries a plastic "pipe" and his gray mouse dangles from his belt. He comes from the city of Hameln on the Weser River near Bremen in the Province of Niedersachsen.

MARKS: "RATTENFANGER//4221.14" seal on box.

SEE: *Illustration 74, page 49.*

THE FAIRY TALE ROAD OF THE BROTHERS GRIMM

In Germany in the middle of the nineteenth century two German brothers were worried that the old oral tales would be forgotten in a world of science and invention. They traveled through the lands between Frankfurt and Bremen collecting oral "fairy tales" from the elders. These "fairy tales" were used to teach lessons to children: good versus evil; morality; the dangers of the unknown; and recounting the legends of heroes and heroines.

Homemade puppets and dolls were part of this long tradition, but gradually doll com-

panies made storybook dolls of many different materials and costumes. Today children can still enjoy the stories and dolls of the Brothers Grimm. The Goose Girl by Goebel was a character in one of the tales.

Goose Girl: 11in (28cm); all vinyl (both the doll and the geese); dressed in simple purple print dress with white sleeves; yellow apron; flat felt slippers; white socks with colored stripes; modeled after the figurine; purchased in Germany in 1987. When purchased these dolls had been discontinued. The book in the picture is Polly's childhood well-worn book of *The Tales of the Brothers Grimm*.

MARKS: "GOEBEL" on metal tag; "M.J. Hummel//C Goebel" on back of neck.

SEE: *Illustration 75, page 49.*

KIS

The picture in the background is the Glockenspiel on the tower of the Rathaus (the town hall) on the Marienplatz the center of Munich. Crowds gather there at 11:00 A.M. each day to watch the figures march around the tower. It was built to commemorate the end of the plague of 1517. The older woman is entertaining her friend from Heidelberg.

Munich Woman (Doll on left): head made of a spongy dark flesh-colored material needle-sculptured over a light mask face; same material used for arms and legs; wooden body; mohair wig; cutout eyes painted black in pupils; dark blue felt dress trimmed in red; beige print apron with red flowers; doll is knitting a blue and maroon scarf; 1960s.

MARKS: None. This is a Kis doll.

Moni, a Turn of the Century Heidelberg Woman (Doll on right): 9in (23cm) all-European hard plastic; very thin mohair wig with braid around entire head; pink and white print dress trimmed in lace; striped white and maroon apron with ribbon and lace trim; carries basket inset with cloth which matches dress; 1980s.

This was made by a doll artist who was recreating the dress of the late Victorian period for the different provinces and/or cities of Germany. She used the same doll with the same hairdo for each province (see *Illustration 72*). These dolls are historical rather than provincial costume dolls.

MARKS: "Figure of doll/Wohellieben" on one side of triangular tag. "Moni" on other side of tag.

SEE: *Illustration 70, page 50.*

(From left to right)

Lüneberger-Heide Region Girl: 7in (19cm); hard plastic; jointed arms and legs; sleep eyes; dark blond floss hair in braid rolled in low bun; red cotton skirt with green braid edging; paler green taffeta apron with red and green rickrack trim; dark green brocade vest with green, yellow and pink fringe; pink and green braid on mid-vest; green cotton bodice; cap matches bodice with lace trim; black ribbon ties; black bow with streamers in back; 1988.

MARKS: "Schneider Original Trachten; Luneberger-Heide Region" on tag.

Franken Mädchen (Frankish girl in Rothenburg Region): 10.5in (27cm); hard plastic; jointed at neck, shoulders, hips; painted facial feature; blond mohair wig in centered back bun; black removable shoes; white stockings; pantaloons; black cotton skirt; brocade green and black apron with gold braid; elaborate trim; black felt vest; white blouse with lace trim; maroon shawl with green print and heavy long black fringe; white net with large oval hat with gold braid crown tied with white ribbon; 1988.

UNUSUAL IDENTIFYING FEATURE: White bonnet.

MARKS: None.

Lüneberger-Heide Shepherd: 5.5in (14cm); all European celluloid-like hard plastic; jointed at shoulders only; Gnome-like caricature face with painted features and applied white fur; black felt trousers, red felt vest with gold buttons; white shirt; dark blue felt cape; black felt hat; 1988.

MARKS: None.

Gura Marburg Region Doll: 12in (31cm); hard plastic; jointed at shoulders and hips; blue sleep eyes with brush lashes; auburn swept back mohair wig; removable black patent shoes; white socks; white net petticoat with lace; green cotton dress with red floral ribbon trim; same trim on sleeves; white taffeta neckerchief; red fedor-type headdress//black satin streamer ribbons, white taffeta apron with lace trim.

UNUSUAL IDENTIFICATION FEATURE: Fedor-type headdress.

MARKS: "GURA" on silver and blue wrist tag.

Stoll Puppen Harz Region Girl: 8.5in (22cm); hard vinyl; jointed at neck, shoulders, hips; dark brown mohair wig pulled into low bun; blue sleep eyes; removable black shoes; floral pantaloons with appliqued hearts at knee; green cotton petticoat trimmed in lace; red linen-weave cotton with heavy red, green, white braid; green brocade apron with red flowers; black satin cumberbund; black vest with green and red embroidery and red fringe; white blouse; gold choker necklace; green brocade squared-off cap which matches apron; black streamers in back.

MARKS: "STOLL" on pin; "Stoll Puppen//Harz Region" on wrist tag; 1988.

SEE: *Illustration 71, page 51.* Barbara Comienski Collection. James Comienski Photographer.

51

STEINER, HERM

Little Red Riding Hood and the Huntsman: 10in (25cm) each; European composition (almost like plaster); excellent color; beautifully painted faces; jointed at shoulders.

Little Red Riding Hood (Doll on left): dressed in Bavarian-type costume; white blouse; black velvet weskit with strings crisscrossing silver buttons; gold skirt; white apron; red shoes; unusual "squared-off" red hood which is often used on both old and new German dolls instead of a cape with a hood.

Huntsman (Doll on right): matching costume; white shirt; black vest trimmed with gold rickrack; gold pants with red pom poms; matching hat; red painted shoes; 1920s-1930s.

Fairy Tale Road dolls.

MARKS: "STEHA (in diamond)" on back of each doll.

SEE: *Illustration 76, page 52.*

Hesse Doll: 17in (43cm); hard plastic; flirty blue eyes; real eyelashes; beautiful flesh tone on face; underneath the bonnet which covers the neck is a top knot of hair (custom in province); large gathered white collar trimmed in lace; striped silk apron with hand embroidery around hem; crepe dress; striped silk apron with hand embroidery at hem; patent leather shoes; 1950s.

This doll is from the Pryor Collection

MARKS: None.

Small Hesse Doll Held by Larger Hesse Doll: 4in (10cm); cloth face; cloth body over armature; mohair wig in top knot; full white collar; black felt bow under chin; cotton apron with black lace; red dress with embroidered ribbon around hem of skirt.

MARKS: None.

SEE: *Illustration 78, page 52.*

Hansel, Gretel, and the Witch: 3.5in (9cm) *Hansel* and *Gretel*; 5.5in (14cm) *Witch*; cloth face with textured paint on face and neck; European composition for body; metal feet wrapped in felt so they can stand alone; late 1930s.

There are many, many dolls portraying the story of Hansel and Gretel. This tiny version was chosen for this book for the miniaturist or those who live in small houses or apartments and need to conserve space. The German toymakers made dolls for everyone. Their creations continue the legends collected and made famous by the Brothers Grimm.

MARKS: None.

SEE: *Illustration 77, page 53. Lavern Ahrens Collection.*

(Dolls from left to right).

Lubeck Testorf Region Lady: 8.5in (22cm); European hard plastic; painted features; dark blond mohair wig in low bun; floral petticoat and pantaloons; appliqued hearts on both knees; maroon taffeta skirt with silver and black braid; white taffeta lace trimmed apron with gold plastic; black velveteen bodice trimmed in lace in asymmetrical pattern; two rows of pearls on left; black round cap with lace trim and ties; removable black shoes; 1988.

MARKS: "STOLL" pin and on gold wrist tag.

Child from Nordfriesland Region: 6in (15cm); European hard plastic; painted features; dark blonde hair in bun; black polished cotton dress with white rickrack and lace trim; lace apron; black embroidered neckerchief fringed with red, green, white floral embroidery; fastened with silver chain and pearls; silver lace choker; half-moon-shaped black headdress with some embroidery; 1988.

MARKS: "STOLL" pin on apron.

Child from Vierlanden-Hamburg Region: 6in (15cm); European hard plastic; jointed at shoulders only; painted features; dark brunette hair in a braided center back bun; red cotton skirt trimmed in white lace; green taffeta apron trimmed in white lace; white blouse; black satin sash; red felt vest inset with gold braid yoke; unique traditional yellow hat tied with black ribbon bow and streamers in back; 1988.

MARKS: "STOLL" on wrist tag.

SEE: *Illustration 72, page 54. Barbara Comienski Collection. James Comienski Photography.*

Hesse Doll (Doll on left): 12in (31cm); European hard plastic; jointed at head; shoulders; hips; upswept brown hair; missing hat; sleep eyes; German provincial costume with red cotton skirt with black trim around hem; white blouse; dark blue velvet dirndl; red heart-shaped neckpiece with five buttons; black patent shoes with buckle; buckram petticoat; tiny embroidered garters hanging down over white stockings; late 1950s-1960s.

The province is sometimes called Schwain-Hesse because the river Schwain runs through the province.

MARKS: "GURA DOLL WITH NATIONAL// COSTUME I OF//SCHWAIN// (HESSE) 23/ 30CMCM" on tag.

Hesse Doll (Doll in middle): 15in (38cm); painted bisque head; cloth body and limbs; blond bangs; hair turned under on top of head; red felt embroidered hat on top of hair; deep flesh tone beautifully painted; rosy cheeks of a German child; white eyelet sleeves attached to heavily embroidered velvet top; heavy red flannel skirt with embroidered trim; heavy stockings; blue cotton apron; black leather shoes; late 1920s-early 1930s.

Armand Marseille is maker of the doll.

MARKS: "A 449 M"//Germany//5/0; "Strobeck" typed and pinned to the back of doll.

Hesse Key Wind Dancing Doll (Doll on right): 7.5in (19cm); hard plastic; blonde doll with bangs

Lady from Hamburg Fish Market: 8.5in (22cm); hard plastic; jointed at head, shoulders, hips; bisque-like coloring; auburn center-part mohair wig with braid crown; black cotton skirt; gold-colored felt vest trimmed in black; white lace-trimmed blouse with jewel broach; rake used to spread fish at harbor market; 1988.

MARKS: "Wohlleben" on wrist tag.

and knob on her head; white sleeves; dirndl with heart and buttons on heart; blue skirt; lace apron; key wind mechanism that makes the doll turn around and appear to be dancing; 1968.

MARKS: None.

SEE: *Illustration 79, page 54.*

Sweetheart Dolls: Key wind dancing dolls made by August Knoch Company.

1. Charles.
2. Indian Boy and Girl.
3. Clown.
4. Tegernsee Girl.
5. English Bobby.
6. Dutch Boy and Girl.
7. Dutch Boy and Girl.
8. Bavarian Girl.
9. Goose Girl.
10. Black Forest Boy and Girl.
11. Princess with Wig.
12. Hessian Girl.
13. Buckeburg Girl and Boy.
14. Hawian Girl.
15. Sailor Girl and Boy.
16. Weihnachtsmann, St. Claus.
17. Tyrolian Boy and Girl.
18. Red Riding Hood.
19. Scotch Boy and Girl.
20. Girl from Franken.
21. Girl from Heligoland.
22. Sleeping Beauty.
23. Carnival Girl.
24. Girl from Bodensee.
25. Cowboy Girl and Boy.
26. Girl from Harz.
27. Vintage Girl.
28. Monk from Munich.
29. Chiemgau Girl.
30. Spreewald Girl.
31. Friesland Girl.
32. Luxenberg Girl.
33. Swiss Guard.
34. Boy and Girl from Rothenburg.

They also made many other types of German provincial and regional dolls.

SEE: *Illustration 79, page 54. Hessian doll* for an example.

Black Forest Region Doll (Doll on left): 11.5in (29cm); all celluloid; jointed at hips and legs; painted facial features; dark brown human hair wig gathered in a pigtail in the back; red velvet jumper top with gold rickrack trim; black collar with gold thread embroidery; white cotton blouse; black taffeta skirt with gold, silver, red trim at near bottom of skirt; red velvet piece at hemline; white tapestry apron trimmed in embroidered ribbon at waist and gold lace at hem. 1900-1920. The company is Rheinische Gummi Und Celluloid Fabrik Co.

MARKS: "Picture of Turtle in diamond//29" embossed on back; it does not have the "Schutz-Marke" or the word "Germany".

The Black Forest Region is a mountainous area in the southwest section of Germany.

This doll is very well preserved for its age and fragility.

SEE: *Illustration 80, page 55.*

The Bodensee Region is an area in the South of Germany where the Rhine River almost forms a lake. It adjoins Switzerland.

German Peasant Girl Gretchen (Doll on left): 8in (20cm); bisque head; painted eyes; closed mouth; five piece, straight leg German composition body; red print head scarf, green felt jacket with braid, blue and black herringbone striped skirt; navy and red apron; all original; circa; 1909.
MARKS: "K★R 114" on back of head.
Bavarian Boy (Doll on right): bisque head; googly eyes; closed smiling mouth; black velvet short pants; white gauze shirt with green tie; multi-colored braid suspenders; circa 1914.
MARKS: "A.M. 323" on back of head; this number sometimes used on *Nobbikid*.
SEE: *Illustration 73, page 55. Shirley Karaba Collection.*

GURA

The Gura Company is one of the better producers of German costume dolls in the modern era. The dolls have excellent quality and color and are well made. The boxes are especially attractive.

As with American dolls of the hard plastic era, these dolls have appreciated in value in the last few years.

Olympic Doll Drei-M-Puppe-Schwesterlein Klein (Doll on left): 12in (31cm); all vinyl; sleep eyes; blond hair in pigtails with flowers in her hair; white blouse; red felt scarf; black felt belt with three Olympic rings; green skirt with embroidery trim; mint-in beautiful box; souvenir of Munich Olympics.
MARKS: "Triple Virticle M" on back.
Bavarian Girl (Doll on right): 12in (31cm); European hard plastic (has a celluloid-like quality); blonde saran wig; black felt hat with gold braid and feather; black velvet weskit with silver chain fastening buttons; white blouse with puffed sleeves; blue scarf with blue fringe which is held closed with a bouquet of flowers; white apron with embroidered heart trim; red cotton skirt with typical Germanic trim around hem; red beads; patent shoes; 1950s.
MARKS: "Gura" on round blue tag.
SEE: *Illustration 83, page 56.*

Bodensee Region Doll (Doll on right): 10.5in (27cm); European hard plastic; sleep eyes; brown mohair wig; jointed at shoulders and hip; white sleeves and neckpiece; black weskit with gold buttons and gold chain; blue print scarf around neck; dark blue taffeta skirt; trimmed with rickrack; unusual straw hat with black velvet around rim; red tapestry ribbons sewn together trim the top of the hat; not original shoes; early 1950s.
MARKS: "GURA: TRACHTEN PUPPEN SPIELPUPPEN" on blue and silver circular tag which can be seen in the picture.
SEE: *Illustration 80, page 55.*

Hofbrau House Squeaker Old Man: 7in (18cm); composition head and body down to waist; squeaker in paper roll body; papier maché feet stamped out by machine; highly detailed molded, and painted face; shirt also molded and painted; loden suitcoat with green felt trim; green overvest; gold felt hat with green button on top; hat stitched with GPC; holds beer stein with letters HB for Hofbrau House, a celebrated beer hall in Munich; 1950s.

MARKS: "Rolly Toys//Made in Western Germany" raised letters under shoes.

SEE: *Illustration 85, page 56.*

Monk of Munchen (Munich): 6in (15cm); all vinyl; black felt robe with yellow felt cross and collar; carries Hofbrau House vinyl mug; sleep eyes; 1971.

Munich was founded in 1158 on the site of a monastery of monks. The monk has become a symbol of the city. This symbol can also be seen on the porcelain beer stein.

MARKS: None.

SEE: *Illustration 84, page 57.*

Bavarian Boy (Doll on left): 6in (15cm); European hard plastic; leather lederhosen (short pants); white shirt; red felt tie; leather, painted suspenders; black mohair wig; tiny green Bavarian hat with large white feather; painted shoes and socks. The leather pants are also painted; 1971.

MARKS: "Garmisch" on tag.

Garmisch Girl (Doll on right): 7in (18cm) in seated position; all cloth with Steiff-like seam down the center of the face; well-painted face; cloth body made in sitting position; low square-neckline white blouse with big puffed sleeves; red weskit with tiny black buttons for thread closing; dark green print skirt with red and white stars and dots; knit stocking; tiny felt shoes; loden green Alpine hat with braid; carries bouquet of mountain flowers; 1930s.

MARKS: "Andexer Werkstatte Kunstgewerbe" in circle on tag; "Handarbeit" in center of circle; "Garmisch-under a mountain peak" other side of tag.

SEE: *Illustration 86, page 57.*

German Provincial Dolls:

Upper Row (Left to right).

Girl from Spreewald (Grub aus Berlin): 6in (15cm); all hard vinyl; sleep eyes; dark hair parted in middle; dressed in red skirt with lace apron and collar; white cotton blouse; white embroidered headpiece trimmed with lace; 1992. Her province is Brandenburg; 1992.

UNUSUAL IDENTIFICATION FEATURE: Unusual wide headdress.

MARKS: "SWEETHEART//SPREEWALD" on plastic container.

Girl from Helgoland: 6in (15cm); all hard vinyl; sleep eyes; pink and white dress and skirt; matching hat with braid down back; gold ornament at neckline; white fringe shawl; 1992. Helgoland is a northern German island; 1992.

UNUSUAL IDENTIFICATION FEATURE: The fringed shawl and squared-off hat with ribbon down the back.

MARKS: "Handmade in Germany by Schmider//Helgoland" on plastic container.

Leipzinger Messe MM: 5in (13cm); entire doll rubbery vinyl; unusual man with world globe for a head; blue felt suit and hat with "mm"; carries a tan suitcase; smoking a white pipe. The province is Sashen (Saxony) in the eastern part of Germany; 1980s.

Leipig is important as a center of the German book industry. Every year it hosts a world-wide book fair. This doll is a souvenir from this fair.

Saxony is an industrial province, and in talking to antique doll dealers, gift, souvenir and doll shop owners, they say that a "provincial costume" does not exist. This little man is the best example of a "provincial doll."

MARKS: "SGB-NR" on plastic container.

The brochure from this company says, "You can have this original Stoll-Weigand folk doll in 90 different costumes and 6 different sizes."

Girl from Schlesien: 6in (15cm); hard plastic face and body; vinyl hands; red print dress; white apron and sleeves of dress; white shawl trimmed with lace; red print matching hat with unusual wide, ribbon hanging down the back; the province is Schleswig-Holstein, a northern province that touches Denmark; 1992.

UNUSUAL IDENTIFICATION FEATURE: The headdress is different with the wide piece on back of the head.

MARKS: "Trachtenpuppen//Wiegand" on plastic container.

Girl from Monschau Eifel: 6in (15cm); hard plastic body; vinyl hands; sleep eyes; red skirt with embroidered trim near bottom; white eyelet apron; black blouse; pink shawl with variegated trim; unusually high white matching bonnet with same trim as around skirt; red wool looped fringe around back of bonnet down to neck; the province is Rheinland Pfalz on the border of Belgium; 1992.

UNUSUAL IDENTIFICATION FEATURE: High bonnet tied under chin with fringe around the top.

MARKS: "Original//Schneider//Trachten//Monschau//Eifel" on plastic tube.

Lower Row (Left to right).

Girl from Markgraflerland (near Freiburg): all hard vinyl; sleep eyes; long dark braids; blue dress trimmed in black which is covered by black apron; large white lace shawl; large black bow with black fringe for headpiece; the province is Baden-Wurttenburg in South Germany; 1992.

UNUSUAL IDENTIFICATION FEATURE: Hairpiece is a large bow with fringe attached to bow and hanging down to shoulders.

MARKS: "Smider//Markgraflerland" seal on bottom of plastic container.

Helgoland Man: 4in (10cm); all-painted bisque; tin well-painted face; jointed at shoulders and hips; yellow cotton pants; blue jacket; striped shirt; sailor-type hat that is long in back; from the island of Helgoland; this island is near Scandinavia and the clothes are more similar to their costumes than to the German costumes; 1930s.

MARKS: "Helgolandian" printed inside small box.

Girl from Pommern: 6in (15cm); European hard plastic; painted face; blonde hair with braided bun in back of head; red skirt with green ribbon trim near hem; white blouse; black weskit; red shawl with yellow rick-rack trim; yellow felt hat with green bow on left side; from the province Mecklenburg-Vorpommern; Northern Germany near the Polish border; 1992.
UNUSUAL IDENTIFICATION: Compared to other German dolls her costume is quite plain; bonnet does not cover hair bun on back of head.
MARKS: "TRACHTENPUPPEN//PUPPEN" seal on plastic container.
SEE: *Illustration 81, page 58.*

Bückeburgerin (Doll on left): 8in (20cm); European hard plastic; gold crown with black ribbon headdress; white blouse with big lace collar; black weskit; red skirt with embroidered trim and lace around hem; green apron with black lace; plastic shoes; gold belt; jointed at head, shoulders, hips; late 1950s-early 1962.

The booklet which accompanies the doll says, "This costume we see around the landscape of Bückeburgerin near Hannover. Formerly it was worn only (on) the festival days. The folded frill around the neck and the little cap with its broad slip knots gives it a particularly fine smart-look.
MARKS: "Original//Schmider//Trachen//ursel//buckeburg//Westlich//von//Hannover" on tag.
Bückeburgerin (Doll on right): 9.5in (24cm); celluloid; jointed at shoulders and hips; headdress has gold ribbon pillbox-type headdress; black ribbon frames head and ties under chin; red cotton skirt with black tape trim; blue apron trimmed with red braid; gold 3-bar ornament ribbon down the front; unusual three bar gold ornament at neckline; 1930s. This is an excellent example of differences in costumes from the same city or region or era. In this case there is a difference of about twenty years. However, the costume can still be identified.
MARKS: "Turtle mark" on doll; "Buckeburgerin" on front of apron.
SEE: *Illustration 82, page 59.*

Bodensee (Doll on left): 13in (33cm); bisque socket head; set brown eyes; feathered brows; painted lashes; accented nostrils; open mouth with four upper teeth; dimples; pierced ears; original blonde mohair wig; jointed wood and composition body with straight wrists; original ethnic costume; beige hat trimmed with red rickrack; red shawl; print blouse; blue apron; 1888 and later.
MARKS: "Bähr & Pröschild 224" on head.
Blonde Bisque Girl (Doll on right): 11.5in (29cm); bisque socket head; blue sleep eyes;

feathered brows; painted lashes; accented nostrils; open mouth with two square upper teeth and one square lower tooth; pierced ears; original blonde wig; jointed wood and composition body with straight wrists; white dress with black jacket; 1920s-1930s.
MARKS: "S4H 719 Dep" back of head.
SEE: *Illustration 87, page 59. McMasters Productions.*

German Peasant Woman: 9in (23cm); composition; picture shown in Romanian Section; probably from Hesse; tall hat over topknot in blonde hair; black jumper with top adorned with gold embroidery and jewelry; white blouse; white skirt with lace insets; carries basket; before 1911 (see *Illustration 186, page 123.*)

Greece

The history of Greece begins at the crossroads of the European and Asiatic continents. There has been constant movement between governments, divisions of the country, religion, and culture.

There are three major land divisions: the North, the South and Central Greece. The Northern division, including Macedonia and Thrace, is bounded by the Olympos mountains. South of Macedonia is Thessaly, a province that is often referred to as a Byzantine area with cosmopolitan influences from both Europe and Asia. Central Greece is south of Thessaly. The Southern division is the island-like province of Peloponnesus. Greece also includes many, many, outer islands.

The pictures of the dolls for the World Crafts Council show the influence of many cultures on the costumes of the Greek people. Each island has its own traditional costumes. The island of Crete is included in this chapter.

All of these dolls were made for the World Crafts Council. They were made from a type of clay pottery using individual molds. Then each was painted and dressed in the various regional costumes of Greece, and tagged by Dora Parissis. A gold seal on the base said, "Made in Greece". The men are 14.5in (37cm) tall. The women are 14in (36cm) tall. Some of the tags are no longer with the dolls, making exact identification difficult. The tagged dolls have their regions identified.

(Dolls from left to right).
Crete Man Carrying Worry Beads: White cotton shirt; black wool vest embroidered in gold; pants gathered and upturned at crotch in the style of the Middle East; red, black, white cloth belt around the waist; white painted stockings; painted black shoes.
Lady: Body padded; white wrap-around scarf tied on top of head; red, blue, gray plaid slim skirt; white cotton overblouse with tiny white buttons; painted black high shoes. She has no tag, but she matches the *Chios* man.
Chios Man: Blue and white plaid shirt; beige wool sash; black cotton pants gathered and folded at crotch in style of Middle East; orange, red, and white scarf tied in back of head; long pointed metal nail on handle clutched in his hand.
Mykonos Lady: White cotton blouse with large sleeves; maroon cotton jumper top embroidered with gold thread; white apron; crocheted apron over other apron; white, filmy cotton skirt; scarf on head looped on right side; low shoes painted black; white painted stockings.
Man from Crete: White shirt with wide sleeves; vest with red trim; black trousers folded and gathered at the crotch; maroon scarf; carries Worry Beads; hat with tassles hanging down. These tassles will fly freely when he dances.
SEE: *Illustration 91, page 61. Louise Schnell Collection.*

Greek Woman (Doll on left): 9.5in (24cm); pressed cloth face; vinyl arms and hands; stiffly packed cloth body; red, white, blue plaid dress with red trim; fleece coat which matches man's cape; dark blue apron trimmed with red, orange, green rickrack; holds raw sheared wool in right arm and uses drop spindle in left to make thread for yarn; fancy embroidered socks; leather shoes with black pom poms; 1960s-1970s.
MARKS: None.
Old Greek Sheep Herder (Doll in middle): 7.5in (19cm); hard molded cloth painted face; mohair whiskers and hair; cloth torso arms and hands; wooden legs; white pants; blue and white cotton plaid shirt; wide black belt with gold chain attached; felt vest embroidered with gold thread; embroidered brown bag hanging from shoulder; black felt tam on head; black leather shoes with black pom poms; carries stick to prod sheep; 1950s-1960s.
MARKS: None.
Younger Greek Sheep Herder (Doll on right): 9.5in (24cm); pressed cloth painted face; mohair wig; vinyl arms and hands; stiffly packed cloth body; white pleated man's skirt; black belt with sequin buttons; white cotton shirt; fleece cape;

red, yellow, green bag over shoulder; black leather
shoes with black pom poms. 1960s-1970s.
MARKS: None.
SEE: *Illustration 88, page 61.*

World Crafts Council
(Dolls from left to right).

Man with Costume Similar to Both Crete and Chios: Black shirt with white stripes; black bolero; maroon sash; folded and gathered pants; white painted boots.

Lady with Blue Striped Blouse and Skirt: Different from other dolls; white apron; black painted boots; head scarf tied on side of head and hangs over shoulder.

Lady from Lesbos: Maroon wool harem pants; white cotton overblouse tied at neck with purple ribbon and tied at waist; white cotton scarf with flowers painted on it tied at top of head; black painted shoes.

Lady with White Embroidered Apron: White blouse; black jacket with rounded neck; red skirt; white bloomers tied at ankles; white painted boots; scarf wrapped around shoulders and hanging down in front and back.

SEE: *Illustration 90, page 62. Louise Schnell Collection.*

Zarkos, a Greek Evzones (Soldier) (Doll on left): 8in (20cm); composition head; cloth body; early 1950s.

A feature of the World Wide Doll Club was a "secret" hidden somewhere on the doll. The "secret" of this soldier is a Greek flag which can be seen in the picture.

Also accompanying the doll was a letter which says:

"Dear Little Friend, I salute you. My name is Zarkos Angisoulakis and the first thing you should know is that I am a Greek soldier. What you will say, a soldier? Then why is he wearing a skirt? I will tell you.

"I am very proud of my costume. It is called the "fustanella" and is the official uniform of the Royal Guards. We soldiers are specially chosen for our bravery from the highlands of Greece and are called Evzones. We are famous for the many battles we have won for our beloved Greece. I come to you straight from Athens and even this minute, while I talk to you there are Evzones dressed like me standing guard in front of the Royal Palace. Every Sunday we parade through the streets of our capital to the Tomb of the Unknown Soldier, and it is a very stirring sight. Our silken tassels swing with our walking and the sun glitters on our braid-trimmed, bespangled jackets and the golden crown of our caps."

The letter is four pages long and tells about the life, culture and history of the people of Greece.

MARKS: None.
SEE: *Illustration 89, page 62. Patricia Moisuk Collection.*
Girl with Spindle by Maria Helena of Portugal (Doll on right): For more information (see *Illustration 180, page 119* in the Portugal section.)

Greenland

Greenland Doll: 8in (20cm); hard plastic; sleep eyes; black wig with topknot and red, white and blue ribbon around topknot; red rayon snowsuit; hand crocheted band around upper torso; red, white, green ribbon belt; black cuffs on sleeves; real white leather boots; white embroidered ribbon trim on upper boots; 1950s.

This is an inexpensive nicely dressed doll.
MARKS: None.
SEE: *Illustration 140, page 96.* (Lapland section).

Hungary

The Danube River is of vital importance to the Hungarian people. It divides the country and the city of Budapest between the hills of Buda and the plains of Pest. Most of the country is flat, but there are sizable ranges of hills in the north and west.

Today it is getting harder and harder to remember that the country was located at the western edge of the "Iron Curtain" which divided the European continent for almost 50 years. Budapest was different than the other Communist countries. It was and still is one of the largest, sparkling capitals of the Eastern European block and the envy of the other Communist countries.

Polly was fortunate to be on the first tour that did not have a Communist tour guide before the fall of the Berlin wall. The people on the entire tour were delighted to be allowed to visit the sights, eat the wonderful food, and talk freely to the Hungarian people in many areas of this country.

During the Communist period Kimport was importing Hungarian dolls and featuring them in their delightful little magazine *Doll Talk*. They advertised several of their Hungarian offerings this way.

"Every picturesque village in this greatest plain section of all Europe had variances of costume detail, different wedding customs and rich traditions of its own. Here are a few ideas gleaned from Kimport research.

"Short skirts and sleeves are worn with a pretty fringed shawl that cross the body at Czinkota. Those shiny jack boots are worn while dancing the wild Csardas and are often handed down as family heirlooms. Embroidered round apron and little mule-like shoes are beloved details in some sections of the Alfold or lowlands; so is the sleeveless bodice. There's a peculiarly pleated flounced or ribbon bound full skirt which is worn around Debreezen. There, the ones for humans, have cardboard strips inserted in the top tucks to maintain that sharply pleated look."

Kimport is no longer in business, and for the collectors interested in costumed international dolls, the authors highly recommend that they search for these little yellow magazines at doll shows, antique shows, and auctions for authentic information about International dolls. Today Kimport dolls are in many museums.

Marga was a Hungarian Company which made excellent quality dolls with heavily embroidered clothes. Many of the dolls were women carrying babies. However, they also did make child and baby dolls. They have a unique art quality which makes them easy to identify. Not only are their faces beautiful, but other details such as exquisite clothes make them a very collectible doll.
Mother: 14in (36cm); papier mâché face; cloth body; mohair wig; white heavily embroidered cap with red ribbons hanging down the back; red metal beads; white embroidered blouse; knife pleated white skirt under heavily embroidered apron trimmed with lace; hand knit stockings; embroidered cloth shoes.
Baby: papier mâché face with mohair wig; white bonnet embroidered in blue; white lace collar; bundled in white blanket trimmed with red embroidery; 1973.

The company was in existence in the 1930s, and one of their dolls has a United States customs paper tag which indicated it was an exhibit at the New York World's Fair in 1939.

The pictured doll was purchased new on December 6, 1973 at the Budapest Conference in Oakpark, New York.
MARKS: "MERET//FOGY AR//MADE IN HUNGARY."
SEE: *Illustration 92, page 64. Anita Siqust Collection.*

Hungarian Girl: 9in (23cm); papier mâché head; cloth body not jointed; pretty painted face; thread wig; white blouse; silk skirt with blue embroidered ribbon near bottom of skirt; real leather boots; red felt vest with rickrack trim; flowered headdress that may mean she is a bride; 1930s.

This is the only doll saved from Polly's childhood. She is shown with a picture of the Castle overlooking the Danube and the city of Budapest. The doll has been hung on the Judd Christmas tree since Pam was five years old.
MARKS: None.
SEE: *Illustration 94, page 64.*

Hungarian Bride (Doll on left): 9in (23cm); painted papier mâché face; stockinette arms; cloth body; thread hair; pink taffeta headdress with multi-colored yarn hanging down sides and back; gold beads at edge of headdress; blue taffeta dress with lace collar, red trim; 12 gold buttons; white cotton sleeves with red embroidery holding in the puffed sleeves; lace at edge of sleeve; white apron with red, blue, black embroidery; yellow ribbon bow; high red leather boots; purchased in Budapest in the late 1970s.
MARKS: None.
Marga Girl with Jump Rope (Doll in middle): 7in (18cm); stiffened cloth mask head; stockinette arms; cloth body; white embroidered blouse and overvest; blue, tightly pleated cotton skirt with pink ribbon trim; white apron with eyelet around edges; heavily embroidered; white stockings with red thread embroidered sparsely; red leather slippers.

Although this doll is not marked, it has all the characteristics of the same embroidery art as the larger Marga dolls (see *Illustration 92, page 64*).
MARKS: None.
Hungarian Groom (Doll on right): 10in (25cm); stiffened painted mask cloth head; bowler-type felt black hat with white band; stockinette arms; cotton body; painted mustache; white embroi- dered shirt; black vest with green stitching and gold beads from the shoulder to the back; wide, white cotton pleated Hungarian long pants; high leather boots; purchased in Budapest in the late 1970s.
MARKS: None.
SEE: *Illustration 93, page 65.*

Hungarian girl: 9.5in (24cm); celluloid head; cloth body.
MARKS: "Made in Hungary" tag on inside of skirt.
SEE: *Illustration 175, page 117. Lois Jean Adam Collection.*

Hungarian Dancing Man (Doll on left): 11.5in (29cm); cloth; painted face; mohair wig; dark red scarf and sash; white cotton shirt; black baggy knee-length pants; leather boots; holding a string of small beads.

Hungarian Dancing Woman (Doll on right): 11in (28cm); cloth; painted face; long mohair wig; yellow cloth hat and sash; white blouse with red embroidery; black weskit with white embroidery; short red silk skirt with white, blue, yellow stripes; white petticoat with red trim; second petticoat with black trim; both showing below skirt; high leather boots.

MARKS: None.

SEE: *Illustration 95, page 66. Nancy Gallagher Collection.*

Hungarian Man: 13in (33cm); painted stockinette face and heavy gauze body; right side-glancing eyes; painted line for mustache; extra pieces of stockinette stuffed with cotton for ears; brown felt wig; arms sewn to shoulders; fingers indicated by stitching only; wire jointed legs which move; white, wide pleated Hungarian men's pants; black apron with white embroidered ribbon trim; embroidered red felt vest; white shirt embroidered in front; faux fur hat trimmed with flowers; high felt boots.

MARKS: "KUBRO//BABA//Made in Hungary" one side of paper tag; "Picture of girl in Hungarian costume//Kubro//Budapest" other side of tag.

SEE: *Illustration 96, page 66. Lois Janner Collection.*

Budapest Girl with Flower in Hand: 15in (38cm); painted bisque head; cloth body and limbs; heavy lines under eyes; red headpiece with ball of white and yellow yarn (almost like pom poms) on top; red print blouse; gold beads around neck; blouse trimmed with green yarn; white multi-pleated sleeves with embroidery; black print skirt with red, yellow, blue embroidered flowers; red tape trim; high-heeled feet; red leather high-heeled shoes; unusual construction of legs with knees; beautiful hand embroidered multi-colored apron; 1920s-1930s.

This is a very unusual doll. A similar earlier doll by Heubach of Koppelsdorf is in the Hungarian National Museum.

MARKS: "Peasant Art//Arts Populaires-Volkskunst//Nepmuvesvzet//Budapest IV." red seal on underclothes.

SEE: *Illustration 97, page 67.*

Iceland

In spite of the name of the country, Iceland is today a popular tourist destination and home to approximately 300,000 people. Most of them are descendants of the Norse people or the Celtic folk from the British Isles. The majority of the population live in the towns, and the cost of living is very high. They do have hot springs that they use to heat their homes.

Although today they wear the clothes of the Western World, they do have traditional Icelandic costumes which are worn at celebrations. They especially wear them for folk dancing.

Icelandic Girl: 17in (43cm); lovely, clear, composition head; long flax braids; cloth body; cream blouse and apron; black dress with weskit top; gold metal decorations; tam-like hat with tassel; 1950s.

This doll was made in Iceland. The composition is made of salt, wood, glue, and paste.

MARKS: None.

SEE: *Illustration 98, page 67.*

The Wee Folk of Ireland

As March 17 draws near, people around the world gather to play and sing the lovely, haunting melodies of the "Old Sod." Ordinary men and women, with and without roots in the Emerald Isle also tell the ancient, time-worn legends of the Sidhe-fold, the wee ones.

Poor in natural resources and captive to a harsh, rainy climate, Ireland is rich in human resources, and culture; both of these aspects are reflected in the dolls.

Like American doll lovers, the Irish troop to the museums to see the old antique dolls. *Illustration 106* is a replicate of a wooden hand-dressed given to a wealthy Irish child in 1735. The original is in the National Museum of Ireland located in Dublin. Its head and body are one piece of wood with a human hair wig, and the legs are jointed. The finely carved face and long fingers are finished with gesso and then painted. The two-piece dress is of green brocade. The undercoat is heavy cotton with an embroidered hem, and there is a quilted red underskirt. The chemise is cotton with trimming at the neck and elbows of Valenciennes lace. The apron and bonnet are made of fine lawn with drawn thread work. Green silk stockings with fashionable clocks complete the costume (see *Illustration 106.*)

The rural and poor children of by-gone days had hand-carved toys and dolls of wood, hair hurlingballs and bone until after World War I.

Today the American traveler bemoans the lack of expensive artist-quality Irish dolls. However, like the fairies of each rainbow, there are small, charming, often handcrafted dolls that can be loved for their own special native quality.

The Jay dolls, made in Dublin portray the native dress in the various counties from a past time. They are collector items no longer made and becoming scarce even in Ireland.

Happily, the wee folk of story, manuscript, legend, and song still remain in the small dolls of various counties. Even the travelers who "rush" through Ireland's gray-green

Icelandic Girl: 15in (38cm); European celluloid head; brown wig with long pigtails; cloth body and limbs; beautiful face; black weskit with gold braid and string for closing; gold braid edging at bottom; white silk blouse; white crepe apron; tam-like hat with long tassel with gold jewelry near the top; black leatherette shoes; 1920-1930 and later.
MARKS: "Kersa//Spielwaren Werkstatted."
SEE: *Illustration 99, page 68. Shirley Karaba Collection.*

beauty can feel the ancient ways as they suddenly see a tiny doll peer out of a cottage window. *Packie and his Mother* were purchased at a remote, beautiful manor house.

Close to the traveler's hotel is a hedgerow, and under it sits a laughing *Jay Leprechaun* with a pot of gold.

Counties in Ireland
Northern Ireland
1. Antrim
2. Armagh
3. Derry
4. Down
5. Fermanagh
6. Tyrone

The Land Called Ulster
The ancient Kingdom of Ulster consisted of 9 counties. They were the present six counties of Northern Ireland plus Donegal, Cavan and Monaghan which are now part of the Irish Republic. For over 2000 years these counties were under the influence of the Scottish, and they had different customs from the other people in Ireland.
Republic of Ireland
1. Carlow
2. Cavan
3. Clare
4. Cork
5. Donegal
6. Dublin
7. Galway
8. Kerry
9. Kildare
10. Kilkenny
11. Laois
12. Leitrim
13. Limerick
14. Longford
15. Louth
16. Mayo
17. Meath
18. Monoghan
19. Neagh
20. Offaly
21. Roscommon
22. Sligo
23. Tipperary
24. Waterford
25. West Meath
26. Wexford
27. Wicklow

Replica of 1735 Child in the National Museum in Dublin: 12in (31cm); for description see Introduction of the Irish Section, page.

The doll was dressed by Louise Schnell. The design in the apron is made by hand-drawing the threads out of the material.
MARKS: None.
SEE: *Illustration 100, page 69.*

Flower Seller of Dublin (Doll on left): 11in (28cm); special composition used by Jay; character doll typical of the street flower sellers who, according to legend, are colorful characters with a ready infectious wit; 1981.

MARKS: "Jay of Dublin" on tag.

SEE: *Illustration 103, page 70.*

Aran Fisherman (Doll on right): 12in (31cm); special composition used by Jay; character doll. A booklet with him says, "Being a seafaring man, he wore clothes of heavy homespun. The Crios was worn below the waist to give him support when rowing. His footwear or 'pampooties' were specially made to withstand the rough seas. He wore the usual beret associated with fisherman; 1981.

MARKS: "Jay of Dublin" on tag.

SEE: *Illustration 103, page 70. Thelma Purvis Collection.*

These two dolls *Packie* (the Irish nickname for Patrick) and his mother, the *Sewing Lady*, are true Irish "Cottage Dolls" made by Slieve Bawn.

Packie (Doll on left): 13.5in (34cm); all cloth; red looped wool hair; home knitted white sweater and tam; blue tweed trousers with a patch (of course); black felt shoes.

Sewing Lady (Doll on right): 18in (46cm); all cloth; black and red polka dot hat and jacket; gray wool tweed homespun skirt; white hand-knit sweater; brown tweed shoes. She is carrying six spools of Irish thread; extra buttons; needles and safety pins.

MARKS: None.

SEE: *Illustration 101, page 70.*

Fisherman: 8in (20cm); all vinyl; black felt pants; hand-knit white sweater and stocking hat; 1979.

There are many dolls such as this one that come home with visitors of the Emerald Isle. His story is sad, but necessary. When a fisherman marries, his wife creates a unique pattern for the sweaters that he will wear whenever he goes to sea. This is so his body can be identified if there is an accident.

MARKS: "Made in the Republic of Ireland// Celtic Toys" on body of doll.

SEE: *Illustration 104, page 71.*

Molly-the-Emigrant: 9in (23cm); bisque head; cloth body; brown velvet skirt and brown tweed cape; basket in hand.

A tag explaining Molly's story came with her. "Molly, a hand-made character doll with these words from the song 'The Green Fields of Amerikay' on her lips and in her heart, the beautiful young woman dressed in a handwoven cape over her Sunday best, leaves her native mountains and glens carrying her purse and trunk, in it perhaps a crocheted shawl and maybe a photograph of her loved ones."

MARKS: "An Irish Turf//Owencraft// Ballyshannon Ireland" tag on base.

SEE: *Illustration 105, page 71. Carlton Brown Collection.*

Irish Boy (Doll on left): 11.5in (29cm); bisque head; ball jointed body; blonde mohair wig; wool black jacket; wool tweed tan pants; wool hand-knitted socks; oil cloth-type white collar; green silk tie; black felt hat with green silk band; 1920s.

MARKS: "Armand Marseille//Germany//390//A 5/0 M." on back of head.

Irish Girl (Doll on right): 11in (29cm); bisque head; ball-jointed body; dark red mohair wig; polished cotton blue and white checked dress; lavender and white striped apron; black cotton stockings; old shoes; 1920s.

MARKS: "Armand Marseille//Germany//390//A 6/0 M" on back of head.

SEE: *Illustration 102, page 72. Dee Cermak Collection.*

The Irish Harpist: 5.5in (14cm) European hard plastic; black mohair wig; buckrum body; black mohair wig; homespun wool dress with red and white trim around the bottom; handknit black scarf; gold harp.

The small Irish harp is still played for singing and dancing at the many festivals and medieval banquets still held in Ireland. The music is beautiful.

MARKS: "Celtic Toys" on the back of the doll.

SEE: *Illustration 108, page 72.*

Brogues and Stockings of Old Ireland: These hand knit stockings with a loop only around the big toe and the homemade leather brogues were the foot and leg wear of the people of the "land" in Ireland in the 1700s and later.
SEE: *Illustration 106, page 74.*

We found him! We found him! Carryng his Pot of Gold.We managed to picture him before he scurried away. But once you have seen him in Ireland, the Leprechaun stays in your heart forever.

Leprechaun: 7in (18cm); papier mâché head; felt over armature; 1979.
MARKS: "Jay" on wrist tag.
SEE: *Illustration 107, page 73.*

Donegal Man: 11in (28cm); special composition used by Jay; cloth body; brown tweed wool walking suit; black tweed wool Irish cap; gray hand knit sweater and socks; felt shoes; blue felt scarf; carries a wood walking stick.

According to the booklet with the doll, "He usually left home during the harvest season in England for work and consequently wore the more conventional dress associated with the other rural parts of Ireland. This was usually the homespun coat and trousers of tweed with a peaked cap."
MARKS: "Collectors//Character Doll//Handmade By Jay of Dublin" on tag.
SEE: *Illustration 109, page 73.*

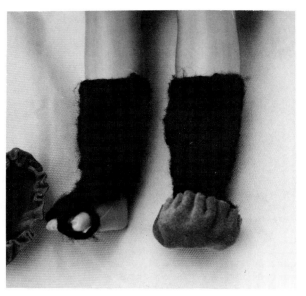

Bisque Irish Doll: 18in (46cm); British ceramic material shoulderhead, arms and legs to knee; red mohair wig pulled back over ears and tied with bow in back; painted face; eye liner; one stroke painted eyebrows; molded open mouth with four teeth; character-type face; cotton body; composition hands; white blouse; black cotton dress pulled back to show maroon petticoat with narrow vertical white stripes; lace half bonnet tied under chin; light tan wool checked shawl with fringe; black silk striped petticoat; well-made underwear; hand-knitted socks; black leather Irish brogues; *Illustration 106, page 74.*

It was the fashion of the period in Ireland to have beautiful petticoats with rather plain dresses. When the weather was nice, the outer dress was tucked up in a pannier fashion.

MARKS: None.

SEE: *Illustration 112, page 74. Sandra Strater Collection.*

Crolly Doll: 11in (28cm) all vinyl; dressed in a green kilt with matching Irish tam with a feather; white blouse with a jabot trimmed with lace; black velvet short jacket; circa 1980s.

This doll is in a picture in the Polish section with many other European dolls. It is the doll on the far right.

MARKS: "Product of the Gaelacht Republic.

SEE: *Illustration 175, page 117. Lois Jean Adam Collection.*

Irish Girl in Red Cape: 6.5in (17cm); white blouse; green dress; black weskit; white apron trimmed in lace; 1930s.

MARKS: "Irish Made//Gabrielle Castlebellingham" on tag.

SEE: *Illustration 175, page 117* (in Polish section). *Lois Jean Adam Collection.*

Sligo Woman of the 1830s: 11.5in (29cm); special composition used by Jay; cloth body; her clothes are homespun as they were in the 1830s; her dress is a dark blue print with vivid pink flowers; her underskirt is a heavy wool for warmth; she wears a hand knit red woolen shawl; dark blue wool kerchief on her head.

Often the ladies' dresses were pulled up in various ways so the underskirts could be seen. Many were heavily embroidered. This one is not.
MARKS: "Collector's Character Doll" on wrist tag; Made by Jay.
SEE: *Illustration 111, page 75.*

Connemara Farm Woman (Doll on left): 7in (18cm); Jay composition head; cloth body; white homespun shawl; red skirt; blue and white checked blouse; 1970s.

The folder which came in her box says "As a rule her long white shawl covered both her head and greater part of her body. It was worn together with the red skirt which was dyed from Madder. The women were well noted for herding and working on the land."
MARKS: "Collector's Character Doll" on wrist tag.
Connemara Woman Leading A Donkey Loaded with Peat (Doll in middle): 7in (18cm); Jay composition head; cloth body; red dotted skirt; red wool shawl; 1970s.

The folder says "When she was home she wore a colored homespun skirt, shawl, headdress and pink apron. As she worked the land, the shores or 'pampooties' made from raw hides gave her feet greater protection from the Rocky Land."

The cloth donkey has two baskets, one on each side, loaded with peat, the fuel used for heat in the cottages.

Connemara is the name given to the western part of Galway. It is a moorland with a sparse population because the land is so difficult to farm, and the people have had a difficult time making a living over the years.
MARKS: "Collector's Character Doll" on wrist tag.

The doll on the right is probably the most popular of all the Jay dolls. Not only has she been purchased by many visitors to Ireland, but she is often found in Irish homes. Ireland is a devout Catholic country, and *Nun* dolls are very popular.

Nun (Doll on right): 7.5in (19cm); special composition by Jay; cloth body; excellent sculpturing on face; nun habit of Irish order; long chain with cross; 1970s.
MARKS: "Collector's Character Doll" on wrist tag.
SEE: *Illustration 110, page 76.*

Italy

Italy is a land of dolls. From tomb dolls of children in ancient times, to the wax creche figures of the Christian churches of the middle ages, to the Art Deco dolls of the early part of this century to the present time, the Italians have loved dolls, and many doll companies have dressed their dolls in provincial or regional costumes.

This book has documented as many of the regional costumes as possible. It has been a daunting task because, like other countries in Europe, the boundaries of Italian provinces have changed. Also, each city, town, village, and family have slightly different ways of interpreting the traditional outfits. However, there are certain characteristics which help the collector with identification.

Regions of Italy

These are the main areas of Italy today. If the doll is old and has a region or city tag, the region or city may not be listed. Only the major cities in each of the current regions are listed.

1. Apulia (in the southeastern area in and near the "heel" of the Italian boot: Bari, Taranto, Brindisi, Manfredonia.)

2. Basilicata (independent state in Rome): Vatican.
3. Campania (southwest on Tyrrhenian Sea): Naples, Pompeii, Vesuvius, Salerno, Sorrento, Amalfi Drive area, Capri, Capua.
4. Dolmonites (Also known as Trentino-Alto Adige) Italian Tyrolean Region: Merano, Bolzana, Cortina d'Ampezzo, Chiusa, Verona, Vincenze, Tirolo, Spondigna, Naturno, Valgardena.
5. Elba Island.
6. Emilia Romagna (east central region bordering the Adriatic Sea): Bologna, Carrara, Ferrara, Modena, Piacenze, Parma, Ravenna.
7. Friuli-Venezia Giula (northeast corner bordering Yugoslavia): Udine.
8. Latium (Lazio): Rome.
9. Ligeria (in northwestern area along the Tyrrhenian Sea): Genoa, La Spezia, Ventimiglia.
10. Lombardy (northwestern section bordering mountains): Milano, Lake Maggiore, Lake Como, Brescia, Cremona, Mantua, Sesse Arunca.
11. Piedmont/Valle d'Aosta: Torino, Turin, Courmayeur, Aosta, Stresa, Trento, Cogne, Bardonecchia, Stresa, Sestriere, Novara.
12. San Marino: Independent state near Adriatic Sea in midwest Italy.

13. Sardinia (Island off west coast of Italy in Mediterranean Sea): Sassari, Cagliari, Oristano.
14. Sicily (The "Boot" of Italy in the southwest Mediterranean Sea): Palermo, Messina, Mt. Etna, Reggio di Calabria.
15. Tuscany (west central area bordering the Ligurian Sea); Florence, La Spezia, Ventimiglia, Arezze, Sienna, Livorno.
16. Umbria-Marches (central-western area south of San Marino): Ancona, Loreto, Pergola, Ascoli, Piceno, Urbino, Gubblo.
17. Venice and Venetian Arc (from Verona to Trieste): Venice, Verona, Udine, Treviso, Padua.

Lenci Cortina D'Ampezzo: 16in (41cm); Laura face; felt head, arms, legs; cloth body; black felt dress with weskit effect on upper part of dress; skirt with gold trim; red felt coat with beige cuffs; blonde mohair wig with braids attached to head with embossed gold pins; unusual black felt high hat; black ribbon with purple and pink flowers with green leaves attached to hat; unusually elegant for folkloric doll; late 1930s-1950s.

Cortina-D'Ampezza has been, and still is, a very chic resort in the Dolomites (Tyrolean) section of Italy. People go there to see and be seen in elegant clothes. The hotels, restaurants, and shops are expensive. Clothing designers and others in the Italian fashion world have chalets there.
MARKS: "Modello Deposito//Picture of Doll//Lenci//Torino//Made in Italy" paper tag. Another heart-shaped tag says, "Cortina D'Ampezzo//Veneto".
SEE: *Illustration 118, page 77.*

Friuli Doll (Doll on left): 5in (13cm); hard plastic head, body, legs; vinyl hands; blonde wig; pink headpiece; blue skirt; white blouse; pink and blue on white print apron; carries drop spindle; all original.

MARKS: "Eros//Friuli" tag on dress.

Sardinia Doll (Doll in middle): 19in (48cm); all felt; face pressed very hard to make it smooth; black hair; painted face; feathered eyebrows; large eyelashes; blue eyes with white semicircle under pupil; blue taffeta scarf; sheer yellow scarf; pink taffeta dress with deep "V" neckline; 3.5in (9cm) yellow taffeta hem at bottom of dress; carrying a basket of oranges; 1930s.

MARKS: "Made in Italy for B.Altman & Company" cloth tag sewn on underskirt.

Sicilian Doll (Doll on right): 10in (25cm); felt face and arms; cloth body; dark red mohair wig; brightly painted dark blue eyes; white dot highlight in right corner of pupil; black eyes; closed mouth that looks like a heart; molded chin; hands stitched to indicate fingers with thumb separate; red and white striped dress; white and yellow trim near hem; white linen apron with yellow ribbon and white ribbon trim; large black head scarf; black felt shoes; late 1920s-early 1930s.

MARKS: "Siciliana//N(75)09//E.N.P.A.L.//Made in Firenze, Italy." on large paper tag stapled to back of dress.

SEE: *Illustration 113, page 78.*

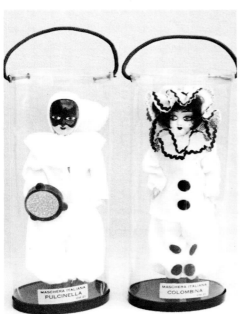

CARNIVAL AND OPERA CHARACTERS

Pulcinella (Doll on left): 20in (51cm); European hard plastic; white clown suit and hat; black mask; carrying a red tambourine; 1960s-1970s.

MARKS: "Maschera Italiana Colombina" tag on plastic container.

Colombina (Doll on right): 8in (20cm); European hard plastic; white girl clown suit and hat; black rickrack trim and buttons; 1960s-1970s.

MARKS: "Maschera Italiana Colombins" tag on plastic container.

SEE: *Illustration 120, page 78.*

These three dolls are all hard plastic. They are part of a series of small hard plastic dolls made by the Lenci Company after World War II. They were identified through a brochure procured at the Lenci store in Milan in the 1970s as well as from their tags.

Girl from Valsarentino (Doll on left): 6in (15cm); all hard plastic; painted face; red felt dress; red and green plaid scarf; white print apron; small black felt "bowler-type" hat; red ribbon trim; gold necklace with heart engraved "Torino."
MARKS: "Lenci Torino" cloth tag sewn into a side seam.

Girl from Calabria (Doll in middle): 8.5in (22cm); waxy European hard plastic; painted face; white cotton blouse; green jacket with ribbon trim; red felt skirt; white rayon apron; missing white lace headdress.
MARKS: "Calabrio" on heart-shaped paper Lenci tag.

Girl from Sardegna (Sardinia) (Doll on right): 6in (15cm); all hard plastic; painted face; white cotton blouse; black heavily embroidered ribbon belt; red felt skirt with blue and gold decoration around bottom; brown felt headpiece (straight piece of material tucked at earring and hanging down the back to the waist); silk print scarf around head under brown felt.
MARKS: "Lenci//Torino//Samughed//Sardegna" paper label sewn into apron.
SEE: *Illustration 119, page 79.*

All three dolls had different quality hard plastic and clothing. The third doll, *Girl from Sardegna*, was probably the most expensive doll. These dolls were made over a period of years, and the hard plastic doll had three or more different lines and sizes.

Hard Plastic Doll Costume Dolls Made by Lenci in the 1950s and 1960s
(Many were made with both boy and girl costumes)

1. Torino
2. Sestriere
3. Stresa
4. Bardonecchia
5. Gressoney
6. Cervinia
7. Courmayeur
8. Cogne
9. Milano
10. Garda
11. Valtellina
12. Valgardena
13. Tirolo
14. Valsarentino
15. Venezia Tridentina
16. Merano
17. Venezia
18. Cortina
19. Friuli
20. Ligeria
21. Riviera Adriatica
22. Bologna
23. Fireze (Florence)
24. Toscana
25. Umbria
26. Marche
27. Lazio

28. Roma
29. Scanno
30. Napoli
31. Capri
32. Sessa Aurunca
33. Calabria
34. Puglie
35. Sicily
36. Sardinia
37. Bersagliere (soldier)
38. Guardia Papale
39. Carabiniere (Policeman)
40. Alpino Soldier
41. Marinaio (Sailor)
42. Sorrento
43. Calabria
44. Abruzzo

Most of the above costume dolls were also made in the 1920s and 1930s as the better-known cloth dolls.

The above information came from a Lenci brochure in the Lenci Company store in Milan in the 1970s. Many of the costumes were from the northern provinces where the company was located.

VENICE CARNIVAL DOLLS

Just before the sober period of lent which precedes Easter, people of many countries in the world celebrate "Carnival", another name for the familiar Mardi Gras. In the olden times people took a vacation from growing crops and everyday work, put on costumes over their warm clothes, hid behind masks and forgot their normal inhibitions. The *Venice Carnival Lady* (doll on right) is wearing an ornate carnival costume.

Gradually the European countries began to outlaw "Carnival" when the fun making seemed to hurt or offend its citizens. A few years ago a group of young people came to Venice and created a renaissance of some of the best of the old customs. They started craft shops to recreate old souvenirs, masks, costumes and dolls. These are not the traditional souvenir shops, but studios where artists and artisans work and create the magic of Carnival before your eyes. The *Harlequin* (doll on left) is one of their creations.

Harlequin in Musical Box (Doll on left): 6in (15cm); chalk-like composition face; well-painted with mask; checkered suit with primary colors; "Jack in the box" apparatus operates the doll; 1978.
MARKS: None.
Venice Carnival Lady (Doll on right): 10.5in (27cm); European hard plastic head and body; vinyl arms; well-painted face; dress style 1700s with ornate white tapestry panniers with gold, blue, red and yellow embroidery over white net ruffled skirt trimmed with gold; red, blue, yellow cloth flowers on skirt, at waist, and on matching felt hat; white mohair wig; 1978.

The Grand Canal and the city of Venice can be seen in the picture.

MARKS: "Made in Italy" on black vinyl shoes.
SEE: *Illustration 116, page 80.*

CONTRADA DELL'ONDA

Palio di Sienna Flag Bearer: 8in (20cm); plastic and vinyl; dressed in blue and white costume with blue and silver trim; 1978.
MARKS: "Siena Italy//Contrada dell'Onda."
SEE: *Illustration 115, page 81.*

History of Sienna's Palio

Sienna is a small town about 30 miles from Florence. The most important annual event for this small town is the famous "Palio dell Contrade". The origin is lost antiquity. The first event is run on July 2.

Representatives of the 17 "contrada" of the town dress up in their own colorful costumes from the middle ages. These costumes can be seen on the poster behind the doll. Each "contrada" has its own colorful banner. The doll collector has his choice.

81

The wearers of the medieval costumes first assemble in the Piazza del Compo and put on a banner-waving show similar to our baton twirlers during the half time of a football game. They do this with ballet-like precision.

Ten representatives of 10 of the 17 "contradas" chosen by lot ride bareback around a small racetrack three times. The horse that completes the three laps (with or without its rider) wins the race.

On August 16th the remaining seven riders compete with three of the original ten riders chosen by lot.

Great celebrations, feasts, huge dinners and torch parades by the winning "contrada" follow for several days.

The "Palio" has been repeated every year for centuries without interruption.

The names of the Contradas are:
First Row (from left to right).
1. Trombetto di Palazzo.
2. Contrada della Chiocciola.
3. Contrada del Bruco.
4. Contrada della Torre.
5. Contrada dell'Istrice.
6. Contrada dell'Onda.
Second Row (from left to right).
1. Contrada della Pantera.
2. Contrada della Lupa.
3. Contrada dell Leocorno.
4. Contrada della Giraffa.
5. Contrada dell Nicchio.
6. Contrada dell'Aquila.
Third Row (from left to right).
1. Contrada dell'Oca.
2. Contrada del Montone.
3. Contrada della Selva.
4. Contrada della Civetta.
5. Contrada della Tartuca.
6. Contrada del Drago.

Castelrotto Girl: 12in (31cm); felt head; cloth body; unusual "fully" stitched hands; elegant black dress with red trim and ribbons; white pleated collar with crocheted trim; 1930s.
MARKS: "Lenci" on round silver tag; "Castelrotto" on flowered tag.
SEE: *Illustration 114, page 82. Nancy Smith Collection.*

Castelrotto Boy (not pictured): 12in (31cm) same body characteristics; wears fleece outer coat; white blouse; red vest; black "Cowboy-type" hat; carries a bagpipe-type instrument; 1930s.
MARKS: Unknown.

Napoli (Naples) Lady with Tambourine (Doll on left): 7in (18cm) papier mâché face; cloth body; vinyl hands and shoes; royal blue cotton skirt; pink ribbon near hem; white apron with yellow ribbon near hem; black weskit; pink ribbons around neck; beige blouse; white felt rectangular headpiece with pink felt stripes tucked near ears and hanging down the back; 1960s-1970s.

MARKS: "Made in Italy//Napoli//47" printed on shield-like tag.

Sorrento Lady Waving Tambourine (Doll in middle): 5in (13cm); pressed felt face; cloth body; vinyl hands; embossed cotton blue skirt with yellow ribbon around the hem; striped belt; yellow blouse with lace collar; lace apron; 1960s-1970s.

MARKS: "Made in Italy//Magis//Roma//Sorrento" on silver tag.

Lady with Basket from the Island of Capri (Doll on right): 7in (18cm) papier mâché face; cloth body; red cotton skirt with green ribbon trim near hem; green apron with piece of white felt sewn on skirt; red flower and ribbon straps; black hair with pigtails rolled into buns on side of head; gold earrings; 1960s-1970s.

MARKS: "Made in Italy//Capri//54" printed on shield-like tag.

SEE: *Illustration 121, page 83.*

Eros Venetian Gondolier (Doll on left): 7in (18cm); stiffened mask cloth face; cloth body; back seam hand-sewn; no ankle seam; mohair wig; 1950s.

Lenci Venetian Gondolier (Doll on right): 9.5in (24cm); hard plastic; purchased in Rome in 1978.

Both dolls are dressed in the typical gondolier costumes; royal blue pants; white sailor shirt with middy collar; blue ties; red sash; straw hat with ribbons. The Eros doll carries a long pole. The Lenci doll carries an ornate white paddle with red decorations. The picture in the background shows one of the lovely bridges over the canal. A tourist boat can be seen on the right hand side.

MARKS: "Eros//Made in Italy" on gold tag. Red Lenci brochure which can be seen in picture; "Lenci" label in clothes.

SEE: *Illustration 117, page 84.*

The most popular Italian costume seems to be the "Roma". It is seen on many types of dolls by many companies and has many variations. Most of the costumes are made of felt. The skirt is generally red with yellow, red, or blue stripes. However, Lenci used green for the base color of the skirt on her *Miniature* cloth doll, but she used red on her tall, vinyl doll. The headpiece is a rectangular piece just off the forehead with lace trim. The white blouse is often seen with black felt cuffs trimmed in yellow. Each of these dolls has a different weskit style. Large gold earrings can be seen on all the women dolls except the tall vinyl Lenci.

(Dolls from left to right).

Magis: The marked *Roman Couple* are unusual and hard to find. They are slightly shorter and chubbier than the regular Magis dolls. They also have a character "smiling" face. Another difference is that they have individual fingers with red fingernail polish.

Magis Man: 8in (20cm); rough pressed felt face; cloth body; glossy bulging eyes are brown instead of the normal blue; thin smiling mouth touches the molded fat cheeks; raised eyebrows; black felt wig like the *Fiori* dolls; red felt jacket; white shirt and tie; faux fur bolero trimmed with green felt; brown felt pants; rough red leather shoes; 1930s.

Magis Woman: Same costume explained above with the following differences; blue glossy bulging eyes; raised eyebrows; mohair wig with pigtails rolled into buns at the side; same sculptured chubby face as the man; white blouse with puffed sleeves; black rough leather weskit with yellow ties; same rough leather turned up shoes as man; 1930s.

MARKS FOR MAGIS COUPLE: "Magis// Made in Italy//Roma" on gold square paper tag; "Map of Italy" on blue and silver second tag.

Lenci: 14.5in (37cm) all soft vinyl; same general outfit with no decorations on blue rayon apron; sleep eyes; synthetic black hair with bun in back; 1960s-1970s.

MARKS: "© Lenci" on tag.

Lenci Cloth Miniature: 9in (23cm); unusual Fiori-type black felt wig with felt braided buns over ears; double row of flowered trim on apron; has all characteristics of Lenci *Miniature* dolls; 1930s-1950s.

MARKS: "Lenci//Made in Italy" ribbon tag sewn in skirt.

Magis Lady: The same costume explained above; usual Magis face with heart-shaped lips and a surprised look on her face; raised tiny eyebrows; one row of felt flowers on green apron.

MARKS: None; tag missing.

SEE: *Illustration 124, page 85.*

Milano (Lombardia) Girl (Doll on left): 9in (23cm); pressed cloth face and shoulder-plate; vinyl body, legs, hands; white rayon blouse; orange weskit with black thread indicating closings; lace collar; blue felt skirt with red ribbon trim around hem; plastic shoes; unique gold plastic one-piece headpiece which represents the pins which were placed in the hair; 1960s-1970s.

MARKS: "Magis//Roma//Made in Italy// Lombardia" on tag sewn to skirt.

Milano (Lombardia) Miniature Lenci Girl (Doll on right): 9in (23cm) pressed felt face; cloth body; dressed in pink felt with lavender and brown felt trim; black felt wig plaited in back; gold pins stuck in head to resemble headdress; beads around neck; embroidered organdy apron with ruffle; pink felt jacket with lavender ties and trim; underclothes have pink rickrack felt trim which makes it a late period doll; black felt shoes; late 1930s-1950s.

UNIQUE IDENTIFICATION FEATURE: Pins in hair in "halo" fashion.

MARKS: None.

SEE: *Illustration 122, page 86.*

Sorrento Man with Guitar: 8.5in (22cm); felt face; cloth hands and body; white cloth shirt; rose felt pants; green felt vest; red felt tie and stocking hat with tassel; variegated colored sash; carrying a guitar; 1960s-1970s.

Music is important in the lives of all Italians, but it is especially important in Sorrento. Very often dolls from that region carry a guitar or other musical instrument.

MARKS: "Magis//Roma//Sorrento" on tag.

SEE: *Illustration 129, page 86. Louise Schnell Collection.*

SWISS GUARDS

The Vatican City since 1929 has been an independent and sovereign state.

(Dolls from left to right).

Swiss Guard with Metal Helmet: 3.5in (9cm); painted head and hair; all celluloid; traditional red, blue, yellow uniform made of ribbons; painted yellow-striped stockings and black shoes; white ruff around neck; long red feather attached to helmet; sword on leather belt carries a pike; 1963.

This is probably one of the most detailed, sculptured, molded, painted, and costumed doll in this book. Even the metal helmet has tiny details in the casting. It is a classic for the miniature collector.

MARKS: "Anchor" molded on the back.

Swiss Guard: 3.5in (9cm); finely molded heavy celluloid; same costume made of ribbons except this doll has a black cloth beret pulled to the right side; carried a pike; cardboard base; 1960s.

MARKS: None.

Swiss Guard Without a Helmet:
4.5in (12cm); molded rigid vinyl;
sleep eyes; same costume made of ribbons; no hat; 1960s.

MARKS: "ROMA" on base.

E.N.A.P.L.: Swiss Guard; 10in
(25cm); all cloth; eyes painted with
glossy paint; long "spidery" eyelashes; molded bump in chin; "Fiori-
type" felt hair; metal pins at shoulder
and hip joints; heart-shaped mouth;
same uniform made of felt stripes
over a felt shirt and knicker-type
pants; blue felt tam; 1930-1950.

UNUSUAL IDENTIFICATION
FEATURE: Glossy eyes and spider-
like eyelashes.

MARKS: None.

SEE: *Illustration 123, page 87.*

Genova Lady (Doll on left): 6in
(15cm); hard plastic head; painted
face; felt body; red floss hair in braids;

blue top; purple skirt; white, red, brown scarf;
candy container; 1953.

An advertisement came with the doll. It says
"...are as beautiful and distinctive as the Italian
provinces that their colorful costumes represent;
hand-made and hand-decorated to the finest old-
world tradition. Available in six different costumes. And in addition each doll is filled with
delicious Italian assorted soft-centered fruit drops.
The dolls, widely acclaimed as prized collectors
items, are ideal for unusual Christmas gifts. Each
doll is $2.98."

People sent their money to the Case Company,
1901 Superior Ave. Cleveland 15, Ohio.

MARKS: "Defour//Genoa" on red tag on front
of doll.

Ventimiglia (Liguria) Lady (Doll on right): 7in
(18cm); paper mâché face and body, vinyl hands;
pretty painted face; braided thread wig with knot
in back; straw hat with black bow on left side
under hat; gold necklace; red and white cotton
skirt with black trim; black faille apron trimmed
with black lace; embroidered felt weskit; white
cotton blouse; vinyl black shoes; 1960s-1970s.

This outfit looks very similar to the French
Nice costume.

MARKS: "Magis//Ventimiglia//Ligeria//Made in
Italy" on tag.

SEE: *Illustration 127, page 87.*

FLORENCE

Many, but not all, of the dolls from Florence, are holding flowers and wearing garden party hats and bright colored costumes. Three of them are shown in this picture. The doll representing Florence in *Illustration 126* is very different.

S.A.G.T. Florence Doll (Doll on left): 8in (20cm); pressed cloth head; stuffed, white cotton body; painted face with side-glancing eyes; bright red lips; mitt hands with separate thumbs; machine stitches on hands to indicate fingers; purple rayon dress with fuschia felt trim at bottom of skirt; turquoise insert in front bodice; doll carries red, white and blue flowers with green leaves. She is missing her wide hat. 1960s-1970s.

MARKS: "S.A.G.T." cloth label sewn into underclothes.

Lenci Florence Miniature Doll (Doll in middle): 9in (23cm); felt head and arms; cloth body; white blouse; red and white skirt; blue apron quilted with special design; yellow and matching blue wide hat; doll holding white daisy-like flowers. Original Lenci box in background; 1930s-1950s.

MARKS: "Lenci" in silver paper circular tag; "Lenci//310/449" on box.

Lela Florence Doll (Doll on right): 8in (20cm); hard papier mâché head; cloth body; vinyl hands; straw hat with green leaf and deep pink flower; green ribbons on her blonde pigtails; white blouse; black weskit; orange flannel skirt; purple, green, lavender, yellow print apron; pink felt trim around apron; plastic shoes; 1960s.

MARKS: "Lela//Creazioni Original//Florence// Made in Italy" tag sewn into clothes.

SEE: *Illustration 125, page 88.*

Sardinian Girl: 14in (36cm); "Lucia" face; felt head; cloth body; orange felt cape trimmed in yellow felt; orange skirt with white appliqued decorations; carrying a wicker basket; black head scarf; 1930s-1940s.

MARKS: Tag missing; this is a Lenci doll.

SEE: *Illustration 131, page 89. Sandra Strater Collection.*

Girl from Sicily: 9in (23cm); felt head, cloth body; festival costume; red felt weskit and skirt with blue and yellow felt trim; lace headpiece fastened in back; large gold earrings; 1930s-1950s.

Like the other regions of Italy, there were variations of costumes in the villages for ordinary wear and for festivals.

MARKS: "Lenci" on round silver tag; "Lenci// made in Italy" on cotton ribbon tag attached to clothes.

SEE: *Illustration 132, page 89. Beverly Findlay Collection.*

Florence is considered to be one of the most beautiful cities of the world. Artists are attracted not only to its beautiful buildings, but they know that Florence has a very special daytime "golden light" that has been captured in this photograph from a hill looking over the city.

Many of the costumes of the dolls of Florence seem to be related to flowers (also see *Illustration 125, page 88.*)

Florence Girl with Watering Can (Doll on left): 7in (18cm); all vinyl; red print skirt; white apron with picture of Firenze (Italian name for Florence); short black felt dirndl with red string closings; white blouse with red straps from dirndl; doll carries copper watering can; straw hat; 1978.

MARKS: "FIRENZE" with picture of city on apron.

SEE: *Illustration 126, page 90.*

This city has a history of the Florentine Soccer Game which seems to go back to the 14th or 15th century. The last of the games was played in 1779, but in 1930 the games were revived. Three games are played each year in ancient costumes. A procession precedes the games, and the doll in the picture

is a trumpeter. At the end of the game the winning team is awarded the Victory Pennant as well as the traditional white calf, and the procession winds its way to the Piazza Santa Marie Novella. Dolls in other costumes are available in Florence (or maybe your local doll show.)

Trumpeter for the Soccer Games (Doll on right): 8in (20cm); European hard plastic head; vinyl body; red and white felt clothing; cape and long stockinette hat; 1978.

MARKS: "Eros//Firenze//Valletto del Comuse//Italy."

SEE: *Illustration 126, page 90.*

Romeo and Juliet: 5in (13cm) each; hard plastic; *Juliet* is dressed in a red taffeta dress with white print underskirt; heartshaped headdress of the period; blonde mohair wig fashioned with long, thick braid; silver belt. *Romeo* wears a felt light green tunic, hat; matching green stockings; white shirt; black felt cape and shoes; both dolls attached to red and black cardboard base; 1978.

Verona is the fabled city of the Romeo and Juliet story. These dolls were inexpensive, but nicely made by Eros.

MARKS: "63//Giulietta//(Verona)" on silver tag.

SEE: *Illustration 130, page 90.*

Naples Couple (Dolls on left): 8.25in (21cm); felt, painted mask faces; back head seam hand sewn with overcast stitches; rounded bulging eyes; glossy dark red, oval lips; raised sculptured eyebrows; applied single piece of felt shaped legs; mitt hand with thread indicating fingers; seam at ankle; felt shoes stitched around the sole for decorative effect; girl wears red skirt, white shirt; striped cape; felt hat; 1930s.

UNUSUAL IDENTIFICATION FEATURES: Seam at ankles and unusual ear on Fiori dolls.

MARKS: "Napoli" on tag. This is a Fiori Doll.

Naples Old Woman (Doll in middle): 11in (28cm); sculptured, molded; pressed felt mask character face; cloth body, hands, legs; brown felt skirt; beige taffeta blouse and specially folded scarf-like headpiece; small black felt weskit with tape closings; red beads; striped beige, red, blue, green apron; ribbed stockings; all original; late 1920s early 1930s.

MARKS: "Giachetti//Made in Italy//NAPOLI" on red and gold tags.

Sardegna (Sardinia) Lady (Doll on right): 9.5in (24cm); felt face, hands, legs; white body; bulging, painted, side-glancing eyes; raised sculptured eyebrows; mohair wig; eye shadow behind eyelashes; two-tone lips; mitt-shaped hands with separate thumb and stitching indicates fingers; no ears; no ankle seams; seams on front and back of legs; red felt skirt and bolero; white blouse; tiny all ribbon weskit; blue apron with ribbon trim; crisscross embroidery on entire costume; 1930s-1950s.

MARKS: None. This is a Magis Doll.
SEE: *Illustration 128, page 91.*

In the early 1930s Mussolini needed money to fund his war. To win favor with the House of Savoy, Mussolini named a new luxury liner the *Conte di Savoia*. This costumed Sardinian doll was for sale in the ship's store for the maiden voyage in November, 1932.

He was purchased by the famous movie star Gloria Swanson, a passenger, for her maid's daughter.

Late in the voyage, a turbine blew a hole in the side of the ship, and the workers in the hold sent word to the captain that they only had about five hours until the ship would sink. A sailor at the last minute managed to get some wet concrete to plug up the hold, and the ship made it into New York.

Lenci Miniature Savoy Boy (Doll on left): 9.5in (24cm); felt head, cloth body; slightly raised eyebrows; black felt provincial coat and boots with orange trim, tan shirt and tan gathered pants; brass buttons; unusual long black felt cap with brim that hangs down his back; 1932.

MARKS: "Lenci//Made in Italy" ribbon tag sewn in back of coat. "Maiden Voyage of the Conte di Savoia" on yellow felt strip down the front of the costume.

Lenci Miniature Italian Mountain Soldier (Doll on right): 9.5in (24cm); same characteristics as Sardinian Doll; khaki uniform with silver buttons; cobbled shoes with spikes for mountain climbing; army hat with red pom pom and feather; felt back pack with rope for climbing; 1930s.

MARKS: None; tags missing.

SEE: *Illustration 133, page 92.*

Small Italian Lenci Miniature Carabiniere (Policeman) (Doll on left, standing in shadow): 9in (23cm) *Lenci Miniature*; felt face; raised, sculptured eyebrows; mohair wig; single stitched ears; tricorn hat with 3in (8cm) feathers on top of hat; symbol of Italy in red, green and white on front of hat; cloth body; navy blue felt uniform with ten tiny gold buttons on front of coat; red felt stripes down side of pants; stripes forming "V" in back with gold ornaments; cobbled shoes; a wood sword made in the Lenci woodworking shop hanging from his waist; 1930s.

MARKS: None; tag is missing.

Large Italian Isotie Carabiniere (Policeman): 38in (96cm); felt molded head; felt body over wire armature; painted eyes and arched eyebrows; large nose; mustache; felt over wire armature body; navy blue wool uniform with red piping down the pants and around the waist; tricorner hat with red, white, green feathers and pom poms at top; navy cape with red lining; weighted shoes; 1950s.

MARKS: "ISOTIE Artistic Dolls/made in Florence (Italy)" tag.

SEE: *Illustration 134, page 93.*

Lady from Molise Bojano: 13in (33cm); pressed, painted cloth face; cloth body; linen headdress with hand crocheted trim; white cotton blouse; black felt weskit, lower sleeves, skirt with gold trim; unique double folded-over green felt embroidered in gold thread apron; carries felt flower and leaf in right hand. Molise Bojano is a city in Lombard. 1935-1940. Childhood doll of owner.

Vecchioni had a very different way of dressing their provincial dolls. They usually used the double apron as their trademark, and many of their dolls have only minor changes in their costumes to indicate regions or cities.

MARKS: "Bambola" on one side of tag; "Molise Bojano//Alberani Vechiotti-Milano" on other side of tag.

SEE: *Illustration 135, page 93. Beverly Findlay Collection.*

San Marino

San Marino is an independent republic completely surrounded by Italian provinces. It is basically a mountain area, and the drive to the top is spectacular.

Girl from the Republic of San Marino: 6.5in (17cm); all vinyl; mohair sleep eyes; dark blue shawl; white blouse; bright red skirt; white apron edged with gold braid.
MARKS: "Picture and Rep. of S. Marino" on apron.
SEE: *Illustration 136, page 94.*

Roberto from San Marino: 8in (20cm); felt-like face; cloth body; red felt hat, scarf, shirt; embroidered ribbon over shoulder; blue felt "knicker-type" pants; 1960s-1970s.
MARKS: "Roberto from S. Marino//MM."
SEE: *Illustration 137, page 94. Shari Gordon Collection.*

Sicily Girl (Third doll from right): 9.5in (24cm); red dress; transparent white shawl; carrying a basket; attributed to Fiori; 1930s.
For picture see *Illustration 175, page 117* in Polish Section.
MARKS: "Made in Italy" on the bottom of both feet.
SEE: *Illustration 175, page 117. Lois Jean Adam Collection.*

Pisa (Tuscany) Girl (Doll on left): 7in (18cm); felt mask face; mohair wig with long braids; hard plastic body; yellow felt hat; blue blouse with lace trim; pink overshirt; blue underskirt; white apron with pink flowers and green leaves printed on it; purchased in Pisa in 1978.
MARKS: "Magis//Made in Italy//Pisa" gold tag on dress.
San Marino Archer (Doll on right): 7in (18cm); all vinyl; royal blue and white medieval costume with cape and hat with feather; doll carries black archer's bow; leather belt; 1978.

His beautiful blue box with scenes from San Marino and Italy can be seen in the picture.
MARKS: "San Marino" on box.
SEE: *Illustration 138, page 95.*

Lapland

The Lapland people live in the very northern part of Norway, Sweden, Finland, the Kola Peninsula, and the north-western area of Russia. Their land is known as Finmark, and they have their own language and culture.

Although they all consider themselves Laplanders, in Norway there are sea, river, and mountain Lapps. In Sweden and Finland there are fisher, mountain and forest Laps. The coastal and forest Lapps have adapted to a more settled life. However, many of them are still nomads.

Reindeer skins and furs are used to make clothing including shoes. They use bright colors so they can be seen in the stormy weather and rescued if necessary. They also use colorful embroidery. Their winter clothing is much heavier than the summer attire.

The cap of the four winds is an old form of headwear which is not often used today. It is made with four long points which are stuffed with reindeer hair. The headband has a knot of colored ribbons hanging to one side.

Another type of distinctive headwear is the conical cap made in six sections. There are many variations of both styles of these hats.

The Swedish men often wear large pom poms on top of their hats (see *Illustration 140, page 96.*)

Women wear a variety of "floppy" bonnets, and some women have an usual shaped hat with a high crown bending forward.

Their clothing suits their life style, but today more and more of them are adapting to modern nordic clothes.

(Dolls from left to right).
Greenland Doll: For information (see Illustration 140, page 63.)
Laplander Girl: 4.5in (12cm); hard plastic; vinyl hands; sleep eyes; bright blue felt dress with bright red embroidery; red felt inset toward bottom; Lapland child's red bonnet with yellow braid and rickrack trim; blue pants with red trim; white scarf; leather turned up shoes; 1960s.
MARKS: None.
Norwegian Laplander Man: 13in (33cm); molded pottery shoulderhead; cloth body; blue and orange felt costume; fur boots; felt streamers hanging from the left side of his hat of the four winds; old Laplander doll in excellent condition; 1920s-1930s.
MARKS: None.
Lapland Boy: 6in (15cm); entirely molded of heavy sculpy-type material; no joints; painted with bright blue suit and pants; red and yellow trim; boots also painted with blue and red; hat of the four winds; points on top painted blue; band around head painted red and yellow; 1960s-1970s.
MARKS: None.
Laplander Girl: 6in (15cm); hard papier mâché head; wood body; vinyl hands and feet; dusty blue tunic and pants with red trim; white scarf around neck; red felt hat trimmed with green and red braid; leather boots with red trim; 1970s.
MARKS: "SAME//Picture of seal in Arctic setting" tag sewn on costume.
SEE: *Illustration 139, page 96.*

Swedish Laplander Boy: 14in (36cm); painted composition head; cloth body; unusual sculptured character face; painted eyes; open mouth with teeth; dressed in bright blue coat trimmed in red; red pants and boots; huge pom pom on hat.

The Swedish Lapland men and boys wear the pom poms on their hats.
MARKS: None.
SEE: *Illustration 140, page 96. Sandra Strater Collection.*

Lapland Couple: 13in (33cm) each; papier mâché face; heavy brushed wool clothes with red and yellow felt trim; girl wears blue felt turtleneck shirt; boy wears cotton turtleneck shirt; belts tied with red, green, yellow and white yarn; real leather high boots; man wears cap of the four winds; woman wears bonnet with flaps; 1930s.
MARKS: "Martha//ABO//Martta//Turku" around circular tag; Lappa//Lainen//Tytto"
SEE: *Illustration 141, page 97. Lois Janner Collection.*

Small Norwegian Lapland Boy (Doll in front): 5in (13cm); heavy felt traditional Laplander clothes; blue dress trimmed with red and yellow stripes; matching four winds hat; black boots.
MARKS: None on doll; "K Produkter Norge" on box.
Swedish Laplander (Doll in back): 12in (31cm); carved wood head; cotton-over-armature body; brown wool costume with bright yellow and red trim; brown hat down over ears; carved wood skill and ski pole; wood burned decorations; 1970s.
MARKS: None.
SEE: *Illustration 142, page 97.*

Lapland Boy on Skis: 9in (58cm); papier mâché character face; navy and blue cotton trimmed with red, green, yellow braid; stockinette mittens; hat of the four winds; 1930s.
MARKS: None.
SEE: *Illustration 143, page 98. Lois Janner Collection.*

Latvia

Latvia has regained independence since the breakup of the Soviet Union. The country borders on the Baltic Sea and speaks its own highly developed language.

The old costumes are no longer worn except for special occasions.

Latvian Doll: 4in (10cm); all cloth; entire outfit crocheted; long blonde hair in pigtails; gold band around head; dark coat with white embroidery; white blouse; 1970s.

The national costume is a brightly woven dark striped skirt with a white blouse; wide embroidered belt; small band around head with colored stitches at top and bottom and an ancient design in front.

Today there are Latvian festivals with folk songs, folk dancing, four-line poems sung to ancient tunes accompanied by ancient instruments.
MARKS: None.
SEE: *Illustration 144, page 98. Thelma Purvis Collection.*

Lithuania

Lithuania is also on the Baltic Sea wedged between Byelorussia, Poland and Latvia. This region is one of the oldest areas to have inhabitants. The people are known for their blonde hair and strength as can be seen in *Illustration 145, page 99.*

Lithuanian Lady (Doll on left): 20in (51cm); all wood; painted face; wire frame wooden hands; crown-like headdress; red blouse with white Peter Pan-type collar; holding green leaves; red, green, white plaid skirt; white embroidered apron; date unknown; 1990s
MARKS: "Anavod//uderpez//zvseque."
Lithuanian Man (Doll on right): 24in (61cm); all wood; painted face; wire frame wooden hands; straw hat; flax-like hair; white shirt; blue and red striped, belted vest with two white buttons; red pants; blue socks; wooden shoes.
MARKS: "Anavod//uderpez//zvseque."
SEE: *Illustration 145, page 99. Laverne Kotty Collection.*

Madeira

Madeira is a Portuguese island group southeast of the Azores in the Atlantic ocean. The Islanders are known for their wine and embroidery.

Madeira Girl: 13in (33cm); European hard plastic head; cloth body; sleep eyes; pigtails tied with green wool; crocheted blue wool hat; long piece of wool decorated with gold thread at top of hat; white blouse embroidered with red crosses; red felt vest, skirt, cape; yellow ties on vest; blue trim on cape; skirt trimmed with yellow, blue, white tape; yellow socks with red trim; 1960s.
MARKS: "Madeira" embroidered on cape.
SEE: *Illustration 146, page 99.*

Description of the Madeira Men's Clothing: The men wear loose, calf length white or linen pants that are gathered into a band or cuff and fastened with white buttons. A broad white or red sash is tied at the waist. Their headdress is similar to the cap the women wear except that it has a

triangular piece at each side; white boots are worn without stockings; no picture.

Malta

Chetta from Malta: World Wide Doll Club Doll; 9in (23cm) stiffened felt head; cloth body; wearing traditional costume called "Faldetta"; great lopsided encircling black cape; black skirt; yellow blouse with lace trim; wide red sash; the special secret was a 1947 Malta canceled stamp; early 1950s.

As with all the dolls from the World-Wide Club, there is a letter from the doll. The letter says:

"Malta is an island near the African coast. Its capital is Valetta. Malta is a small island not much bigger than Nantucket, but it has 5000 years of history and its own language. The people are called Maltese, and they trace their history back to the ancient Phoenicians. We are a proud colony of Great Britain so we also speak much English.

"Long ago Emperor Charles V, head of the Holy Roman Empire, gave our island to the Knights of Malta. Soon after they arrived the Suleiman of Turkey attacked Malta. The Knights resisted fiercely and finally won.

"The women of Malta swore a sacred oath that if God would grant victory over the Turks, they and their descendants would wear this costume for 200 years. Today, almost 400 years have passed, but we still wear it - not all the time, but always on holidays and fiestas."
MARKS: None.
SEE: *Illustration 147, page 100.*

Monaco

Monaco is a tiny "fairy-tale" principality on the Mediterranean Sea between France and Italy. Currently, it is ruled by a Prince who married Grace Kelly, a noted American society figure and movie star who died in a tragic automobile accident.

During her reign, she and the Prince established the Monaco Musée National which has become one of the most famous and beautiful doll museums in the world. It features large automatons and other dolls of the past. Its *Santon* collection is excellent.

Monaco Palace Guard: 8in (20cm); all hard vinyl; white felt uniform trimmed with red; red hat trimmed with white; carrying a gun under his left arm; 1985.
MARKS: None on doll; "Monaco" on box.
SEE: *Illustration 148, page 100.*

The Netherlands (Holland)

The Netherlands conjures up images of windmills, tulips and wooden shoes in the minds of most people. This region is well known for its brightly decorated regional costumes and wooden shoes, or *Klompens*, which have been part of Holland, now the Netherlands, for centuries.

As the 20th century nears its end, Western clothing has replaced most of these lovely, traditional Dutch costumes. Today the clip-clop of wooden shoes on cobblestones is heard in remote areas or in tourist centers designed to preserve the old styles and costumes of the Dutch.

Since the costumes are so distinctive, there have been many dolls made with wooden shoes and authentic Dutch outfits. These dolls will also help preserve this vanishing heritage.

Most of the dolls in Dutch outfits are from three regions: Voldendam, north of Amsterdam; Marken, an island in the old Zuider Zee, and the Zealand provinces near Belgium by the North Sea. The authors were lucky to find a candy box doll with twelve pieces of chocolate. Each piece is wrapped in paper with a picture of a provincial costume on it.

This is a very unusual treat purchased in the Netherlands. It combines a regional doll with twelve pieces of chocolate packaged with pictures of costumed dolls of the other regions of the Netherlands.

Illustration 149, page 101 (from left to right).
Row 1: Friesland; Groningen
Row 2: Drenthe; Overijssel
Row 3: Flevoland; Gelderland
Illustration 150 (from left to right).
Row 1: Utrecht; Noord Holland
Row 2: Zuid Holland; Zealand
Row 3: Noord Brabant; Limburg
Union of Haarlem, Flevoland Region Doll: 7.5in (19cm); hard plastic; jointed at neck, shoulders, hips; blue sleep eyes; blonde mohair braided wig; black felt dress; wooden shoes; white cotton apron with blue and red stripes; gold cotton vestment with embroidered weave; white lace bonnet with ruffles; 1990.

MARKS: "FLEVOLAND" on tag on front of dress.
SEE: *Illustrations 149 and 150, page 101. Barbara Comienski Collection. James Comienski Photographer.*

Voldendam Couple: 10.5in (27cm) each; bisque faces; composition bodies; brown mohair wigs; jointed at neck, shoulders, hips; 1920s.

Girl (Doll on left): White lace hat with a pointed top and two pointed side wings called "bulletie"; black blouse with square embroidered collar; red beads; multicolored flannel skirt; apron with flowered top and black flannel at bottom; black stockings; wooden shoes.

MARKS: "Germany 390" on back of neck.

Boy (Doll on right): The men of Voldendam wore distinctive outfits; wide black felt trousers with two large silver buttons; red and white striped shirt; jacket is also black with two buttons; red neckpiece decorated with gold ball; tall fur cap called a "ruigie"; black knit stockings; wooden shoes; 1920s.

MARKS: "Germany//A390M" on back of neck.

SEE: *Illustration 152, page 102.*

Voldendam Dovina Girl: 7in (18cm); hard plastic; head and torso in one piece with downcast head; painted coquettish character face; jointed at shoulders and hips; hard plastic shoes; same costume as the Voldendam doll in *Illustration 152*.

MARKS: "Dovina//Made in Holland" printed on box.

SEE: *Illustration 153, page 102. Sandra Strater Collection.*

Man from Zuid-Beveland (Doll on left): 7in (18cm); hard vinyl head, hands; black vinyl suit and bowler-type hat; red bandana-type scarf held together at neck with small string of beads; silver buttons on belt; black and white striped shirt; carrying vinyl pig; 1970s.

Edi Dutch Doll (Doll on right): 7in (18cm); celluloid; sailor-type tall black hat; black wide pants with two silver buttons on band of pants; red shirt with "V" neck; white insert with red trim; wooden shoes; 1960s.

MARKS: "Zuid-Beveland" on base. "Edi" on tag.

SEE: *Illustration 154, page 103.*

Delft Queen: blonde wig with pigtails; black top with trim around neckline; embroidered ribbon around neckline; red beads with two gold buttons; white and multi-colored striped skirt under an organdy apron trimmed with rickrack; wooden shoes; small lace cap; carrying baskets of fruit.

MARKS: "Lucky Doll//B (horseshoe//W//made in Holland//Delft Queen."

SEE: *Illustration 155, page 103. Lois Jean Adam Collection.*

Hera Girl (Doll on left): 12in (31cm); composition doll from Zealand; dressed in black except large multi-colored scarf-like collar; tight white collar around her neck; wooden shoes; 1930s.

Nederland (Olanda) Boy (Doll in middle): 7in (18cm); hard plastic painted face; blonde thread wig; brown hat and scarf; red cotton shirt; blue trousers; wooden shoes; 1973.

Hera Boy (Doll on right): 12in (31cm); dressed entirely in black; cap-like head piece; 1930s.

MARKS: Both Hera dolls are marked "Hera" on paper tag. Middle doll is marked "Eros//Nederland//Olanda."

SEE: *Illustration 157, page 104.*

Dutch Sailor Smoking a Pipe: 24.5in (61cm); papier mâché head and shoes; cloth body; 5in (13cm) black Dutch hat; orange felt double-breasted jacket; with black cuffs, belt; scarf around neck trimmed with green felt; smoking a genuine meershaum pipe.

This is a large doll, and the shoes really look like wood. However, they are cleverly made of papier mâché so the large doll will not be so heavy.

MARKS: None.

SEE: *Illustration 156, page 104.*

Girl from Zuid-Beveland (Doll on left): 10in (25cm); bisque socket head; composition body; glass eyes with long dark lashes painted under the eyes; open mouth with inset teeth; white underblouse; black weskit under a blue print flowered scarf tucked into her skirt; black skirt; striped blue and white apron; 1920s.

UNUSUAL IDENTIFICATION FEATURE: Unusual lace headdress adorned with gold knobs and two gold plates which measure 2in (5cm) by 3in (8cm).

MARKS: "R 13/0 A" on head. This doll was made by Recknagel.

Girl from Marken (Doll on right): 8.5in (22cm); bisque socket head; sleep eyes; open mouth with teeth; composition body; jointed at shoulders and hips; unusual mixture of contrasting floral and checkered materials; 1920s-1930s.

The hat is sometimes called a "Fairy Tale Hat" and is associated with tales of magical and mischievous elves. The undercap is linen with an over panel of red gauze and lace. The top of the hat is made of red flowered chinz edged with flowered tape. Her red and tan flowered bodice has a contrasting flowered front covering or plastron. Her skirt is blue with a red band. The apron has a checkered top with a contrasting band. the colorful and contrasting floral outfit makes this a very different costume.

MARKS: "GERMANY//390//A AND M" on head.

SEE: *Illustration 151, page 105.*

Dutch Doll (Doll on far left): 9.5in (24cm); all cloth; crocheted hat; wig with long blonde pigtails; white blouse; blue weskit; multi-striped skirt; wood shoes.

Doll attributed to Netherlands.

MARKS: None.

SEE: *Illustration 175, page 117.* Picture in Polish Section. *Lois Jean Adam Collection.*

Norway

The Scandinavian people as a whole are very interested in their past culture, particularly their costumes. Norway folk dress is said to be the most elegant of Europe with its splendid embroidery. Costumes are treasured and handed down from generation to generation. The embroidered parts usually do not touch the skin, and great care is taken when they are worn to not get them dirty or spotted.

Because of their mountainous landscape, many people live in isolated villages. The costume instead of being provincial may belong to a village, a church group, or a particular trade. Today the most popular costume for men is the Telemark style, and for the women it is the Hardanger dress.

In Norway beautiful character and costumed dolls from the different Norwegian provinces and villages of the time were made by the famous Ronnaug Petterssen Company from the 1930s into the 1950s. Their list of provinces from an old advertisement includes: Fana, Gudbrandsdal, Hallingdal, Hardanger, Romsdal, Setesdal, Sunnmore, Rogaland, Vesteelmark-Heddal, Trondelag, Valdres, Vestfold, Osterdal, Nordland, Finnmark (Norwegian Lapland), Karasjok-Kautokeino.

A head scarf with pictures of Norwegian costumes purchased in Norway in the 1970s has a different list (see *Illustration 158, page 108.*) Some of the names are different. These may be the villages in the valleys.

There are companies in Norway today who are continuing to make the traditional costumes. There is also a trend for a cottage industry in a village or town. The undressed dolls may be purchased, and hand dressed and sold in their own shops, hotels and inns. The doll in the white dress in *Illustration 163, page 107* is such a doll. It was dressed in Lillihammer and sold in a hotel shop. It actually is the costume of the village of Lom in Gudbrandstal.

Girl from Vest Agder (or possibly Sunnmore) (Doll on left): 6.5in (17cm); plastic; jointed at shoulders and hips; blue sleep eyes; dark blond mohair wig; white cotton blouse; red felt vest with silver sequins for beads; silver marriage broach; black felt skirt with red and green bands at hem; matching trim on black fringed shawl; white kerchief cap; black removable shoes; painted stockings; 1990s.
MARKS: "Souvenir Produkter//AS//Norway."

Girl from Romsdal Region (Doll on right): 7.5in (19cm); molded felt face with painted features; cloth body over armature; blonde mohair wig; black felt cap; white cotton blouse and apron; navy blue felt skirt; red embroidered felt vest; red stockings; black shoes; 1950s.
MARKS: None on doll.
SEE: *Illustration 160, page 106. Barbara Comienski Collection; James Comienski Photography.*

Bisque Hardanger Girl (Doll on left): Bisque shoulderhead; painted blue eyes; single stroke brows; closed mouth; molded and painted hair; cloth body with bisque lower arms and legs with molded boots; original Hardanger costume; white blouse; red felt vest; bead trim.
MARKS: No marks visible because costume is stitched on.
Swiss Guard Costume Doll (Doll on right): Bisque socket head; set brown eyes with no pupil; single stroke brows; open mouth with four upper teeth; original mohair wig; crude five-piece composition body; original dress uniform of Swiss Guard.
MARKS: "1,12/0" on back of head.
SEE: *Illustration 162, page 107. McMasters Productions.*

There are lovely waterfalls around every turn in the mountain country of Norway. These two dolls have been enjoying the view. Both were purchased in Lillihammer; doll on right was dressed locally.
Small Girl (Doll on left): 4in (10cm); European plastic; blue dress, similar to the Finnmark dress; blue hat, apron, and shawl; red trim; wearing gold brooch; 1977.
MARKS: None.
Girl in White Dress (Doll on right): 12in (31cm); hard plastic head; cloth body; white felt costume with green, pink, brown trim; white hair pulled back with a bonnet; white blouse; gold brooch; black shoes; 1977.

This dress is very similar to the Lom (Gudbrandsdal) dress in *Illustration 169.* The difference is in the color.

In many parts of Norway a girl is given a gold brooch representing the sun on her wedding day.
MARKS: None.
SEE: *Illustration 163, page 107.*

This silk scarf was purchased by Thelma Purvis when she visited Norway (Norge) in the 1970s. It is one way to identify the costumes on your dolls. Provinces and villages are (from left to right):

Line 1: Vaga, Telemark, Setesdal, Valdres.
Line 2: Sunmore, Trondelag, Finnmark.
Line 3: Osterdal, Hallingdal, Hardanger, Lom.
Line 4: Nordfiord, Nordland, Sogn

SEE: *Illustration 158, page 108.*

A Nissi is an imaginary gnome or elf who inhabits the farms and farmhouses of Norway and other Scandinavian countries. He is a mischievous "being" who helps, and hinders, around the farm. If something goes wrong, it is easy to blame Nissi. He makes his rounds at night watching over the household.

Christmas is Nissi's special time. After all his name is a nickname for St. Nicholas. He demands that porridge be set out for him on Christmas Eve or there will be no gifts on Christmas morning.

In spite of his tricks, he is really a "jolly" old Nissi who wishes everyone in the world will have a "God Jul" on Christmas day. Sweden and Denmark share and enjoy the Nissi.

Nissi: 12in (31cm); 15in (38cm) with hat; felt mask face sculptured with a "mischievous" character smile; "stiffly stuffed" cloth body with a "little round belly"; red felt hat and coat; green felt vest with yellow felt trim and red stitching; green and red plaid pants.

MARKS: "RONNAUGG PETTERSSEN" on blue and gold round tag.

SEE: *Illustration 159, page 109.*

Poster to the left of Nissi: This is an old 1930s advertisement for the Ronnaugg Petterssen Com-

pany. In the upper left is the Setesdal couple (see *Illustration 167*); On the left side (from left to right is the *Sunmore Girl, Heddall Girl, Romsdal Girl*. In the center is a *Hardanger Couple* (see *Illustrations 161, page 109, and 169, page 111*). *Barbara Comienski Collection.*

At the bottom of the picture is a blue and white drawing of the Laplander dolls made by the company; (see Lapland section).

Bunad Paper Dolls
Norwegian Provincial Costumes (From left to right):
Row 1: Vestfold, Rogaland, Hitterdal, Setesdal.
Row 2: Austagder, Romerike, Hardanger, Finnmark.
Row 3: Sogn, Valdres, Nordland, Voss.
MARKS: "Printed in Norway."
SEE: *Illustration 165, page 109.*

Hardanger Girl: 16.5in (42cm); molded felt face; inset blue glass eyes; cloth body; blonde mohair wig; small headdress on back of head; cotton body; white cotton blouse; black felt skirt with green felt trim; red felt "V-shaped" vest with seed bead trim embroidery; white cotton apron; black felt shoes with silver trim; 1930s.
MARKS: "Created by Ronnaug Petterssen" tag on dress.
SEE: *Illustration 161, page 110. Lois Janner Collection.*

The Hardanger costume is one of the best known of Norway's provincial costumes. It has been altered very little since the early 19th century except the waistline has been lowered, and the skirts that were originally dark blue are now black.

No book of Norwegian dolls would be complete without a few Trolls. Trolls have been popular with children and collectors for at least 35 years. They are considered cute, droll, funny.

In reality, they do not have this meaning to the Norwegian people. These are representations of "evil" in the world. They are depicted in Norwegian statues and dolls as ugly, menacing, and scary. It is the trolls that cause the problems in everyday life.

The dolls in the picture were carved from wood in Norway and brought to the United States in 1962.
Girl (Doll on left): 6in (15cm); green dress; has "flirty eyes" to get men into trouble.
Old Man (Doll in middle): 7in (19cm); walks with a cane, and his troublemaking is almost over.

Boy (Doll on right): 5.5in (14cm); a "come-on" smile for the ladies, young and old.
MARKS: None.
SEE: *Illustration 164, page 110. Thelma Purvis Collection.*

This picture of a deep valley was taken in a pass in the mountains while driving between Norway and Sweden. In older times, the villages were very isolated. Different costumes and customs were a way of life. The dolls on the left are Norwegian dolls. The doll on the right is a Swedish doll.

Norwegian Hardanger Boy (Doll on left): 9.5in (24cm); all hard plastic; painted face; jointed at neck and shoulders; white mohair hair; black felt hat; bright red jacket with buttons on each side; felt green jacket with red twill trim and yellow embroidery; white felt shirt with a high collar; black felt pants with red stitching down the side; white stockings; plastic shoes; 1950s.
MARKS: "Ronnaug Petterssen" on big circular tag.

Norwegian Lom Village Girl from the Province of Gudbrandsdal (Doll in middle): 10in (25cm); European hard plastic; sleep eyes; embroidered vest with deep "V" neck; matching blue skirt with same embroidery at the bottom of skirt; matching embroidered bonnet but no ties; gold broach of married girl; 1993.
MARKS: "LINDTVED//Made in Norway" seal in plastic container.

Swedish Rattvik (area of Dalarma) Boy (Doll on right): 12in (31cm); painted European composition head; blonde carved and molded hair; black felt "beanie-type" hat with red pom pom on top; white shirt with blue embroidery on cuffs; black felt vest trimmed with red felt; yellow cloth pants; blue felt stockings; black felt shoes with silver decorations; red pom poms attached to black ribbon; the Swedish man's costume often included yellow pants; 1930s.

Actually this costume was a popular Scandinavian style for men in many regions of Norway and Sweden.
MARKS: None.
SEE: *Illustration 169, page 111.*

This picture was taken in Lillihammer, Norway in 1977, the 150th anniversary of the city. This statue had been erected for the occasion to represent the strength and industry of the people of their city. Norway is poor in natural resources, but they are hard workers and have managed to have an excellent standard of living. The small doll at the bottom of the picture came from Lillihammer and illustrates the strength of the lumbermen who still are supplying wood for export. The reader can also get a look at the Norwegian love of dolls from the dolls in the store window.

In 1994 Lillihammer hosted the Winter Olympics. This is a small town, and it was a magnificent undertaking for them.

Lumberman Sawing Wood: 5in (13cm); all carved wood doll; dressed in black woodsman clothes; 1977.

MARKS: "Lillihammer" on base.

SEE: *Illustration 166, page 112.*

Ronnaug Petterssen

Artist Ronnaug Petterssen was born in the northern part of Norway. She studied in Germany and Spain. When she returned to Norway, she was convinced that dolls should be her primary artistic medium. She consequently opened her doll studio in Oslo in 1934.

After endless research in museums, libraries, and Handcraft Associations, and with interested individuals, she achieved her goal of making appealing dolls in provincial costumes. She found it impossible to recreate all the details in dolls of this size, but she retained what was important. She used assistants who were experts in their particular speciality.

The dolls were shown in a Paris Exhibition in 1937 and at the World's Fair in New York of 1939-1940. She also made a small speaking tour in the eastern part of the United States.

Ronnaug Petterssen Doll

Hallingdal Region Boy and Girl (Dolls on left and right): 16.5in (41cm) each; molded felt faces; inset glass eyes; cloth body; blonde mohair wigs. *Boy* has black wool knickers with silver buttons and red and green embroidery; white cotton shirt; red wool vest with silver buttons; white wool jacket with red, green, blue, maize embroidery, red trim silver buttons; red and black wool cap. *Girl* wears black wool jumper; bodice and hem has heavy crewel multicolor floral embroidery; black cotton apron with pink rose print; white blouse with silver button; red stockings, black buckle shoes; embroidered cap; 1930s.

MARKS: None.

Girl from Setesdal Region (Doll in middle): 7.5in (19cm); hard plastic; jointed at neck, shoulders, hips, blonde mohair wig; legs painted black; white lace-trimmed blouse with black bead buttons; black felt skirt with red, green felt deep trim; red and green braid sash; black kerchief with pink roses and green foliage; 1960s-1970s.

MARKS: None.

SEE: *Illustration 168, page 113. Barbara Comienski Collection. James Comienski Photographer.*

Couple from Setesdal: 12in (31cm); molded celluloid shoulderhead with a character face; side-
glancing eyes; dimples; deeply molded curly hair;
all cloth body; wired arms; 1930s.

Girl (Doll on left): Short felt skirt with green and
red felt trim around bottom of skirt; wool petticoats and bloomers with black trim showing below skirt; white blouse; embroidered ribbon trim
belt and straps; black headpiece with ribbons
down the back; colorful striped shawl; arms
crooked to join with her partner.

Boy (Doll on right): Black felt hat; white cotton
shirt; black felt long pants with green stripe; green
felt top with silver bottoms across top; long, red
and yellow decoration from top down to pants;
embroidered ribbon at bottom of each pant leg is
same pattern as the girl's ribbon trim.

MARKS: None.

SEE: *Illustration 167, page 113. Sandra Strater
Collection.*

113

Poland

Poland has many beautiful costumes and interesting customs accumulated over the years. Their location at the crossroads of the East and West have caused them to have been invaded many times over the centuries. Some of the customs of the invaders were adapted by the Polish people. However, through it all, the people of Poland have kept their love of freedom. Their dolls are beautiful and incorporate this longing for independence.

Polish Girl Washing Wooden Dishes at Fence (Doll on left): 7in (18cm); face and hands very hard modern composition; cloth body on armature; pink print skirt; blue short embroidered coat; white kerchief on her head; standing at fence made of sticks; 1970-1980s.
MARKS: "Cepelia//Lalki Regionalne//Hand Made."

Man Costumed as if He Were Riding a Horse (Doll on right): 6in (15cm) high; all hard vinyl; elaborate red costume with vinyl horse's head trimmed in gold; man wears red scarf lined in gold; fancy elaborate beard; gaudy pointed hat; painted eye makeup; hands and high-topped red boots are carved of wood as is the horse's head with its fancy plumes.

The doll named *Laj Konik* represents the persistent efforts of the Polish people to keep their independence over many centuries. According to the information from Kimport which came with the doll, "This is a one man parade float being 'got up' in fantastic Oriental dress." These brilliant-hued and ornamental toyers frisk about the Krakow market square on special festival days in commemoration of ancient Tartar invasions.
MARKS: "LALKA LUDOWA//LAJKONIK// SPORDZIELNIA PRACY//REKODZIETA LUDOWEGO I ARTY STYCZNEGO IM ST. WYSPIANSKIEGO W KRAKOWIE", on base.
SEE: *Illustration 170, page 114.*

This type of costume can also be found in the Catalan Region of the Pyrnees between Spain and France.

Polish King Zygmund August (Doll on left): 12in (31cm); wood pulp composition; coat is brown and gold "glitter" material; white fur collar; matching head-piece with medallion in center; gold necklace; yellow stockings; 1977.
MARKS: "Lalki Regionaline//Krakow" on base.
Queen Barbara Radziwell (Doll on right): 9.5in (24cm); papier mâché face; gold and white brocade gored high-waisted skirt; gold and brown embroidery in yoke; brocade hat trimmed with gold; 1977.
MARKS: "Lalke Regional//Barbara Radziwell//Hand Made//W. Krakowie-Al Katarzyny" on base.
SEE: *Illustration 171, page 115. Carlton Brown Collection.*

Velvalee Dickinson was a doll dealer on Madison Ave. in New York City. Among others, she imported international dolls and sold them in her shop and through mail orders. She had a thriving business. Her story as a spy is well known and has been told many times in magazine articles and in books. She was finally convicted and served a jail term (see *Illustration 172, page 115*).

The dolls pictured were in her last shipment which happened to be from Poland. They were not the *Mountain Man* and *Bride* pictured, but they were two of the "few types other than pictured." These dolls are beautiful and very well made. *Illustration 173, page 115,* is one of her last advertisements.

...T DOLLS FROM THAT ONCE PROUD AND HAPPY NATION. MA...
...MMUNITY GROUP THAT WAS BOMBED EARLY IN THE WAR. T...
...T OF DOLLS LEFT POLAND BEFORE WAR CAME, HOWEVER, T...
...LD MANY WEEKS AT A TIME IN SEVERAL PORTS, AND JUST...
...). ONLY A SMALL PART OF OUR ORIGINAL ORDER SURVIVE...
...ROUGH EXAMINATIONS IN VARIOUS COUNTRIES WHERE THEY...
...TAINED. THERE ARE A FEW TYPES OTHER THAN PICTURED...
...ES TALL - $5.00 EACH (A FEW IN PAIRS ONLY)

Mountain Man and Bride: 12in (31cm) vivid painted papier mâché heads; cloth bodies; individual stitched fingers; hand made clothes with excellent detail; 1942.

Bride (Doll on left): 12in (31cm); flax wig with long pigtails; white blouse; pink satin vest heavily embroidered with multi-colored beadwork in both the front and back; beige cotton skirt printed with pink flowers; ribbons tied around waist; same type of shoes as her bridegroom; 1942.

Man (Doll on right): Linen tunic; red flannel pants above ankles; Oriental leather upturned toe on his shoes with ties up the ankles; beige leather belt with a pattern of nailheads; felt cape heavily embroidered in red and green; red and green pom poms around neck; large leather pouch around neck decorated with red and gray beads; black fur hat lined with red felt; 1942.

MARKS: "Made in Poland" on cloth tape sewn into *Bride's* costume; "Goral//Poland" on *Bride's* wrist tag. "Hucul" on *Mountain Man's* wrist tag. Both wrist tags were hard to read.
SEE: *Illustration 174, page 116.*

Spring Custom Dolls: 4.5in (12cm); Polish composition head, legs, arms; cotton over armature body; 1960s.

Semus or Dyngus is a spring custom popular in Poland when people douse one another on Easter Monday. It comes from an ancient pagan rite when water was believed to have invigorating power.

Polish Boy (Doll on left): Dark blue high bowler hat with red trim; white shirt; blue tunic with red and blue trim; red pants with green trim; holding a wooden water pitcher.

Polish Girls (Dolls on right): red skirts with stripes; apron with dark border with flowers; red kerchiefs on head.
MARKS: "Cepelia//Made in Krakow" tag on board.
SEE: *Illustration 176, page 116.*
Louise Schnell Collection.

(Dolls from left to right).

Netherlands (Dutch): For more information see *page 105 and Illustration 175, page 117.*

Ukrainian Man: For more information see *Illustration , page.*

Hungarian Girl: For more information see page 65.

Polish Girl: 12in (31cm); papier mâché painted face; straw-like hair; white blouse; white "burlap-weave" material with rows of multicolored flowers; wreath of flowers in hair; red shoes; 1920s-1930s.

MARKS: "SPOEDZIELNIA PRA (BAJKA W LUBLINIE o ZABAWKARSKA" in a circle tag with a stylized doll in center of circle of words.

SEE: *Illustration 175, page 117. Lois Jean Adam Collection.*

Italy Doll: For more information see *page 94 and Illustration 175, page 117.*

Irish Crolly Doll: For more information see *page 74.*

Irish Doll with Red Hood: For more information see *page 74.*

Krakow Girl with "Square" Headdress (Doll on left): Same characteristics as Cepelis doll; red skirt with black stripes around hem; red vest with black trim centered with red strip and six buttons; white print apron with red cherries; headdress is trimmed with embroidered red and blue ribbon which is wrapped around neck and hanging down to the middle of her skirt; black boots; 1960s-1970s.

MARKS: None.

SEE: *Illustration 177, page 117. Louise Schnell Collection.*

Lalki Region Girl: 4.5in (12cm); composition head, hands, legs; cloth body; blue skirt with multi-colored stripes in lower part of skirt; carrying tiny beads; thread wig pulled back in pigtail; 1950s.

MARKS: "Lalki//Regio P//Nalne" seal on bottom of base.

SEE: *Illustration 178, page 118.*

Polish Bagpiper: 14in (36cm); papier mâché painted face; straw-like hair; leather body; burlap tunic and pants fringed at bottom; clay bagpipes covered with blue material; 1920s-1930s.

MARKS: "Tatra//Slavic Fine" mark on tag.

SEE: *Illustration 179, page 118. Carlton Brown Collection.*

Gabrielle Castlebellingham's Small Doll in Red Cape: (second from right) see *page 74 and Illustration 175, page 117 . Lois Jean Adam Collection.*

Polish Peasant Woman: 9in (23cm); composition; heavy beige shawl tied under chin; black lace top over pink top; green pleated apron; blue print skirt under apron; illustration shown in Rumanian section; before 1911.

SEE: *Illustration 186, page 122. McMasters Productions.*

Portugal

History tells us that the "Age of Navigation" started in this small country with King Henry the Navigator sending out explorers to confirm the tales that the fisherman brought back from their journeys. Fishing was and is a major occupation in this small European country facing the ocean.

The statue in the background of this illustration is a huge stylized ship. Henry stands on the prow leading a host of explorers, statesmen, and people starting off on the journeys that eventually enriched the country and led to the discovery of America. (**SEE:** *Illustration 182,* page 120.)

Portuguese costumes are not as elaborate as some of the other European countries. The men often wear rough coats, stocking hats, and tight-fitting pants. The women often go barefoot, and their dresses are less ornate than their aprons.

The people are a happy people who, like the Spanish, love music and dancing. The dolls reflect their way of life.

The Maria Helena dolls have been popular in Portugal for many years. Many of these dolls were sent around the world, especially by companies that sold international dolls by mail order such as the Mark Farmer Company of El Cerrito, California. One of their sales magazines advertised the following:

1. **The Spinning Shepherdess:** A classic pose and job in Portugal. She is busy with her spindle while she watches the flock. 5.5in (14cm). For a picture of this doll (see *Illustration 85,* page.)

2. **The Harvester:** This lady with her straw hat is often seen in the South of Portugal, in the province of Alentejo and elsewhere in Europe. She carries a sheath of wheat; 9.25in (24cm).

3. **The Herdsman:** This one is from the famous region of Ribatego where fighting bulls are raised. 5.5in (14cm).

4. **The Vegetable Seller:** A most charming little peddler, with a loaded wicker basket on her head. The fruit or vegetables contained therein are handmade. 5.5in (14cm).

Girl with Book: 5.5in (14cm); felt over poseable armature; yellow hair; red hat; white top; blue jumper; leather shoes with red bows; holding a book. October, 1959. She is pictured with her yellow book and her white box.

MARKS: "Mascottes Maria Helena" on gold tag on dress.
SEE: *Illustration 180,* page 119. *Mary Elizabeth Poole.*

Farming Couple Taking Their Produce to Market: Lady 7in (18cm); Man 7.5in (19cm); unusual European hard plastic head, hands, legs; cloth body; excellent workmanship; legs weighted to stand alone; 1950s-mid 1960s.

Lady (Doll on left): red and white cotton print blouse; red and green wool plaid skirt; white, blue, red cotton print apron; black ribbon sash; painted shoes; wicker basket on head filled with green yarn and molded vegetables made from the same material as the doll.

Man (Doll on right): blue and white checked shirt; black felt pants; black felt stocking cap with red felt trim and pom pom; carries two dark wicker baskets filled with pieces of green yarn and strawberries.

MARKS: "MADE IN PORTUGAL" tag attached to clothes on both dolls. The boy also has "Sintra No. 142" stamped on sole of shoe.

SEE: *Illustration 181*, page 119. *Lois Janner Collection.*

Girl with the Seven Petticoats (Doll on far left): 5in (13cm); vinyl; multi-colored plaid skirt; bright print apron; unusual scarf tied in the back; holds a basket on her head; is barefoot as is customary. This is a tiny doll, and it must have been difficult to sew so many petticoats on such a small doll. However, they are all there. This is a popular doll for visitors to bring home. It comes in many price ranges; 1968.

MARKS: None.

Fisherman from Nazare (Doll on left): 8in (20cm); cloth doll on wire armature which makes him poseable; blue plaid shirt; black pants and hat; barefoot; carrying a large net; 1973.

MARKS: "Maria Helena" on tag. A booklet came with the doll.

Musical Couple (Dolls on Right): Each doll is 10in (25cm); vinyl; the girl is dressed in a green print skirt; white blouse in a design which matches the ornate black and white apron; red scarf with a basket on her head with large wool pom poms. The man wears black pants; a multi-colored shirt; blue scarf at the neck; and the standard stocking hat. He holds a guitar while the lady dances; 1968.

MARKS: None.

SEE: *Illustration 182*, page 120.

Romania

Romania is another of the eastern European states which has frequently been invaded and conquered throughout the centuries. It borders Moldavia on the east, Yugoslavia and Bulgaria on the south, Hungary on the west, and Ukraine on the north. It is also spelled Rumania.

Many of the costumes of the country have an oriental influence. The shoes often have upturned toes, and the designs are often geometric. The heavily embroidered clothes also feature crochet work. Their costumes vary from east to west, and often are very similar to those of the country closest to the Romanian borders of regions, town or villages.

(Dolls from left to right).

Man in Sheepskin Coat:
13in (33cm); European hard plastic; vinyl hands; white homespun cotton tunic and trousers; yellow embroidery on sleeves and hem of tunic; highly decorated and painted, sleeveless sheepskin jacket; fur around the collar and down the front of the jacket; carries an axe for cutting wood; molded felt hat with brim; painted shoes; wide, brown leather belt with gold chain; black hard plastic shoes; unusual plastic stand; 1960s.

He represents the district of Transylvania in the north eastern section of Romania.

Both Romanian men and women wear variations of the sheepskin coat.

MARKS: "RUMANIA" on stand.

Man with Bagpipe: 13in (33cm); European hard plastic body and hands; mustache painted on face; brown thread wig; high fur hat; white homespun pants and tunic top; hand crocheted lace at edge of tunic and sleeves; white embroidery on tunic; black hard plastic shoes; carries bagpipe made of leather and wood; 1960s.

MARKS: "RUMANIA" on stand. "Coop,//Arta Crissana Oradea//Papusa: Laran Rm. Sarat//Simbol:C XVi 241//N.T. 7043//Pretul; 701ei" printed tag on bottom of stand.

Romanian Lady Carrying Yellow Pottery Jar: 9in (23cm); European hard plastic face, hands, legs; auburn thread wig under black cotton embroidered scarf; cloth handspun; white blouse embroidered in red; embroidered red skirt with red stitching near hem; wide heavily embroidered belt; black apron; sleeves heavily embroidered near bottom; 1960s.

MARKS: "ROMANIA" on stand; "Coop., Arta Crisana Oradea//Papusa Taranca Lapusului//Simbol; c xvi351//N.T. 403-76//Pretul 75 lei" printed tag on bottom of stand.

Romanian Lady with Bag: 9in (23cm); hard plastic face and hands; lovely painted face; unusual embroidered crocheted small hat with two corners; white embroidered dress and jacket; wide blue belt with gold embroidery; blue plaid pleated apron with zig zag stitch around hem; oriental yellow, turned-up-toe shoes; white stockings with thread around them to tie shoes to body; bag for shopping; 1960s.

MARKS: "ROMANIA" on stand; "Arta Crisana Oradea//Papusa Taranca Haleg//Simbol: C XVI 348//N.I. 7043-76 Pretal: 75 lei" tag on stand.
SEE: *Illustration 184,* page 121.

The mate was an Oash girl which "shows a rainbow of colors in her handworked bodice and collar, lace edged apron and trim on long skirt. Her braided dark hair is capped with a Balkan looking red scarf with a print design."

Before and immediately after World War II there were several doll companies that imported excellent international dolls. Kimport was one of the best. As airplane travel made the "world" more accessible, people began to travel more frequently and purchase their own dolls. There was no longer a need for mail order companies so eventually they closed down.

Romanian Dancing Man: 8in (20cm); European-type of hard plastic; wood stick in his hand; long white tunic with fancy embroidery; colorful ribbons around neck and waist; glittery crystals hanging from hat which shined when he danced; late 1960s-early 1970s.

The man is dressed in the national folk dance costume called "Calusarii." The wooden stick he holds in his hand is used to interpret various gestures and motions pertaining to the dance.
MARKS: None.
SEE: *Illustration 187, page 122. Jean Horton Collection.*

Girl Companion to Dancing Man (Not pictured): 8in (20cm); wears national costume called the "Bistrita Nassaud" worn primarily by peasant folk of the outlying districts on holidays and special occasions; white skirt; fancy striped apron; lacy puffed sleeves; elaborately decorated bodice; headdress is a beaded hat with earmuff-like flaps at temples.

This group of dolls was auctioned off by McMasters Productions. They were accessed to a museum in 1911. So all the dolls are older and some would have been made in the late 19th century. They are all 9in (23cm) tall; made from an early form of European composition; single stroke brows; accented nostrils; closed mouths; cloth or cloth over armature bodies; dressed in original native costumes of the represented country; excellent details and in good condition. (Dolls from left to right).
1. Austrian peasant woman.
2. Soviet Union peasant woman.
3. Romanian man.
4. German peasant woman.
5. Polish peasant woman.
For more information about each doll, refer to the country section of the book.
Russian Man: Probably Oash *Farm Man* with white suit with fringe edged cuffs; tam-like hat with red braid on top; cloth pouch hanging from

Vlaska Girl: 12.5in (31cm); European slightly waxy smiling composition head and hands; cloth body; floss brown hair; white blouse embroidered in red and gold; white cotton skirt with red stitching at bottom for decoration; red apron with black striped trim; black homespun over skirt heavily embroidered in diamond and striped pattern; leather oriental shoes with upturned toes and ribbon ties; 1960.

This doll was ordered from Kimport located in Independence, MO, by the present owner, and the doll was advertised in the January/February issue of their monthly little yellow magazine *Doll Talk.*
MARKS: None
SEE: *Illustration 183,* page 121. *Lois Janner Collection.*

Kimport ordered an Oash district *Farm Boy* "resplendent in an all white suit with fringe edged cuffs and sleeves. Color is added by rows of red and yellow trim, embroidered shoulder designs and a funny cloth pouch with rich hued braid straps that hang suspended from his neck, pointed leather shoes and a straw hat with green ribbon trim."

straps with metal decorations; heavy woolen coat; tam-like hat with red braid on top.
MARKS: None.
SEE: *Illustration 186, page 123. McMasters Productions.*

Romanian Gypsy: 16in (41cm); celluloid over metal (often called tinheads); glass eyes; closed mouth; arms look like carved ivory, but are probably celluloid; bisque half-legs with high-heeled feet and painted garters; cloth body; black wig; Gypsy-type dress; Gypsy-type scarf tied at side; red cotton skirt with rickrack and ribbon trim; green felt vest with beads sewn on it; beige blouse with lace trim on collar; two sets of old beads; geometric triangular band at waist line; bracelet on left wrist; very well preserved doll; 1920.

Rich Romanian costumes are decorated with beads, spangles, metal, silk threads and other beautiful and expensive trims. The decorative effects often have a Slavonic geometric pattern. This and other parts of the clothes date back to the occupation of Romania by the Ottoman empire.
MARKS: "Curved Minerva Shield under word 'Minerva'". Minerva was made by Bauschow and Beck.
SEE: *Illustration 185, page 124.*

Russia and the Soviet Union

It has been difficult to decide how to put these dolls in an international category. The break-up of the Soviet Union was swift and still is not completely settled. For convenience, the dolls from the Soviet Union, except for Estonia, Latvia, Lithuania are placed in this part of the book.

Boyar Doll: 14in (36cm); painted, jointed, egg-shaped, wooden head; hard stuffed linen body; tall Russian fur hat; one-piece tunic with wide silver and gold tapestry at top and around the bottom; maroon velvet coat with brown velvet lapels; beige suede collar with gold mesh epaulettes; 1900-1914.

A Boyar was a landed aristocrat in the time of the Czars. The beautiful hand-painted character face has weathered the years well.
MARKS: None.
SEE: *Illustration 191,* page 124.

Romanian Bride (Doll on left): 11in (28cm); bisque face; open mouth with four teeth; sleep eyes; composition hands; cloth body; brilliantly dressed; scarf headdress with blue stripe across back; heavy coins around neck; gold beads around neck; heavy gold embroidery on black weskit; embossed gold cloth apron with red stripes and red wool fringe and gold embroidered ribbons at hemline; under skirt of batiste with blue stripe (same material as skirt) with yellow jewels; oriental shoes with toes pointed upward; hand knitted red stockings; 1920s-early 1930s.
MARKS: "Armand Marseille//Germany//390."
Constanze Lady (Doll on right): 12in (31cm); waxy European composition head and hands; cloth body; blonde floss hair; white blouse trimmed with black braid with tiny loops; some black embroidery on blouse; pleated white linen skirt with hand crocheted lace; black apron edged with braid with tiny loops; pattern on lower part of skirt sewn in gold thread; black shawl over head hides braids; 1960.

This doll is made by the same company as the doll in *Illustration 183,* page 121.
MARKS: "Romania" on stand; "Constanza Rumania" written on paper by person who originally purchased it. The paper was from the Istanbul Hilton Hotel.
SEE: *Illustration 188,* page 122.

124

Girl from Soviet Union (Doll on left): 7.25in (19cm); stockinette face; peg wooden body; spoon hands; blond mohair wig; print dress with puffed sleeves; straw hat; painted shoes; 1930s.

MARKS: "Made in Soviet// Union//5201 Girl" cloth tag sewn to undergarment.

Small Soviet Boy (Doll in middle): 4.5in (12cm); composition head and body; red thread wig; blue checkered tunic; black pants; cloth boots; 1930s.

MARKS: "Made in Union" sewn to trousers.

Ski Girl (Doll on right): 7.5in (19cm); gauze sculptured face with bead eyes; stuffed armature body; pink ski suit; wooden clogs; 1930s.

MARKS: "Made in Soviet Union//8220//Sky-Girl" cloth tag on back.

SEE: *Illustration 190, page 125.*
Shirley Karaba Collection.

Russian Bride (Doll on left): 14.5in (37cm); same facial and body characteristics; bridal crown of multi-colored flowers with multi-colored streamers hanging down in back; white embroidered blouse with short, wide sleeves; dark red tunic with blue trim and gold buttons; red and blue plaid skirt; white underskirt with tiny hand crocheted trim; striped rectangular apron; red stockings; red leather shoes; all original; 1910 into the 1920s.

Russian Bridal Groom (Doll on right): 15.5in (39cm); Russian dark socket head bisque (not as smooth as the German or French bisque); sleep eyes; feathered eyelashes; open mouth with four teeth; human hair wig; wooden bodies jointed at neck, elbows, wrists, hips and knees; white Russian-style overblouse with red rectangular piece down the front; blue, very full, knee-length Russian pants; wide pink silk sash at waist; black stockings; leather black shoes; 1910 into 1920s. The hat is probably missing. Otherwise he is all original.

MARKS: None.
SEE: *Illustration 192, page 125.*

Modern Tea Cozy (Doll on left): 18in (46cm); waxy Russian vinyl face; white hair; white blouse with red trim; blue skirt; red apron with same trim as blouse. Purchased in Moscow in 1992. *Sandra Strater Collection.*
MARKS: None.
Old Tea Cozy (Doll on right): 14in (36cm); stockinette face; red thread hair; dark blue skirt with yellow and orange circles; white blouse and apron with ruffle at hem; white scarf with painted flowers on the ends; 1930s. *Shirley Karaba Collection.*
MARKS: None.
SEE:*Illustration 189*, page 126.

Russian Boy: 7in (18cm); stockinette head and body; carved wooden legs; beige tunic; dark blue pants; painted legs; gray sash; 1930s+.
MARKS: "Made in Soviet Union//Ziormra (Hard to read)"
SEE: *Illustration 194*, page 126. *Mary Tanner Collection.*

Uzbechka Boy (Doll on left): 7in (18cm); stockinette body and head; painted face; red underpants; beige cotton tunic; yellow, red, black striped jacket; yellow kerchief on head; woven clogs; 1920s-1930s.
MARKS: "Made in Soviet Union//8067//Uzbechka" cloth tag sewn to trousers.
Belorussia Lady (Doll in middle): 7in (18cm); all stockinette head and body; painted face; red print cotton dress with pleats at bottom of dress;

heavy beige cotton coat; brown wool head scarf; woven straw shoes; 1920s-1930s.

MARKS: "Made in//Soviet//Union//Belorussia" on cloth tag.

Lady in Red and Yellow (Doll on right): 7in (18cm); all stockinette head and body; painted face; carved wooden legs; looped black yarn sewn on head for hair; red overblouse; pleated red print skirt; yellow shawl; painted wood shoes; 1920s-1930s.

MARKS: "Made in Soviet Union//8091 Ziqamra" on cloth tag.

SEE: *Illustration 195, page 127. Shirley Karaba Collection.*

Russian Nesting Dolls

Nesting dolls have become very popular with collectors of International Dolls in the last few years. With trade between the United States and Russia becoming more open, some very sophisticated "art" dolls are now available.

Nesting dolls celebrated their 100th birthday in 1984. It is generally believed that these small dolls derived from the wooden eggs that the Russian peasants made at Easter for many centuries. About 1884 a set of wooden Japanese dolls came into the hands of the Russian art patron Savva Mamontov, and he commissioned a Russian version of the doll.

For many years Zagorsk, a village north of Moscow, was the center for making this type of doll. Many sets are still made there, but artists in other villages are also now producing these hand painted sets.

There are four sets shown in this book. One is from 1909 and has been well played with by the owner's family. The second is from the Russian Pavillian of the New York World's Fair in 1939. The third group was made in 1993 and shows the different costumes of the various provinces of the former Soviet Union. The last is a 1993 "art doll" of the last Russian Royal family.

Nesting Dolls 1909: Five dolls given to owner; pastel coloring. The colors are very dull from use over the years.
SEE: *Illustration 196*, page 127. *Private Collection.*

Nesting Dolls 1930: Four nesting dolls purchased at the New York World's Fair in 1939. The colors are very bright.
MARKS: None.
SEE: *Illustration 197*, page 127. *Private Collection.*

New Russian Nesting Dolls
(Dolls from left to right).
Siberia Doll: 3in (8cm); wood; hand painted by an artist; yellow hair; red babushka; white dress; red apron and base; three dolls in set; 1993.

Siberia is in the far east of Russia.
MARKS: None.
Ural Mountains Doll: 3.5in (9cm); wood; hand painted by an artist; blue babushka; yellow hair; orange dress with large white flower with green leaves; five dolls in set; 1993.
MARKS: None.
Ukrainian Doll: 4.5in (12cm); wood; hand painted by an artist; black hair; orange and white babushka; orange and white dress with fancy trim with diamond shapes around base; seven dolls in set; 1993. Ukraine is on the borders east of Poland and Romania.
MARKS: None.
Brest Doll: 4in (10cm); wood; hand painted by an artist; red babushka; green dress with yellow flowers and green leaves; red trim around hem; three dolls in set; Brest is southeast of Moscow near the Ukrainian border; 1993.
MARKS: None.
Yashkar: 4in (10cm); Muslim doll; yellow babushka; white dress with red trim; three dolls in set; Yashkar is southwest of Moscow; 1993.
MARKS: None.
SEE: *Illustration 198* page 128. *Michael Policopf Collection.*

Czar's Family Nesting Dolls: Seven dolls in a nest; 7in (18cm) the largest; 1in (3cm) the smallest. Each doll has a hand-painted portrait of the last Czar (1894-1917) and his family. The first doll is the Czar. The next doll is Czarina Aleksandra Federovna (formerly Alix of Hesse in Germany. The other portraits are in descending order from the oldest to the youngest. The daughters (Grand Duchesses) Olga, Tatiana, Maria, and Anastasia, and finally the Czarevitch (heir) the only son Alexis.

The entire family was assumed to have been assassinated in 1917 at the beginning of the Com-

munist Revolution. However, recently there has been some doubt about the deaths of two of the children. 1993.

MARKS: "*НИКОЛАЙ* ".

ГРЯлНЬ//ТЙ artist's signature.
SEE: *Illustration 199, page 129. Sandra Strater Collection.*

Lady from Smolensk: 13in (33cm); stockinette well-sculptured face; red, white, cloth body; red, white, gray "Mother Hubbard-type" dress with green and yellow bands at hemline; dark blue skirt with red band under main dress; white print blouse with red cuffs; red head scarf with multi-colored stripes at ends.

The ladies of Smolensk enjoyed bright colors in their simple dresses.
MARKS: None.
SEE: *Illustration 193, page 129. Shirley Karaba Collection.*

Ukrainian Man (Doll on left): 11in (28cm); entire body made of creamy Russian vinyl; gray fur high Cossack hat; white shirt with red embroidery down front; red wool pants; black high leather boots; 1960s.

MARKS: None.

Russian Smoking Doll (Doll on right): 6.5in (17cm); plastic head and arms; cloth body; character face; dressed in the traditional Russian Cossack style; white shirt with red trim; high gray fur hat; royal blue pants; multi-colored tie belt; doll has open mouth and a pipe that can be smoked; 1967.

This doll was purchased in the Russian Pavilion of the Montreal Exposition in 1967.

MARKS: None.

SEE: *Illustration 202,* page 130.

Lady with High Hat (Doll on left): 10in (25cm); painted stockinette face; mohair wig; white overblouse; gray, red, blue, white, print long skirt; white apron with two rows of ruffles edged in red; high red print headdress with piece of pink fringed wool hanging down back.

MARKS: "Made in Soviet Union" tag on doll.

Doll Sitting Down (Doll on right): 11in (28cm); painted stockinette face; cloth body; red head scarf with black polka dots; maroon weskit with tie closings; red and white skirt; white apron.

MARKS: None.

SEE: *Illustration 203,* page 130. *Shirley Karaba Collection.*

Willage Boy (Doll on left): 15in (38cm); well-sculptured, painted cloth face; all cloth body; beige linen tunic; stencilled trim; brown twill coat and matching hat; brown pants; white stockings; woven straw shoes with ties up to knees; flax hair; rope over shoulder and around waist which ends in a peg; after Communist Revolution. *Dee Cermak Collection.*

MARKS: "Made in S.Soviet Willage Boy" cotton tag.

Willage Boy (Doll on right): 15in (38cm); well-sculptured, painted cloth face; all cloth body; beige linen tunic; stencilled trim; brown twill coat over shoulders; top of hat matches coat; band is lighter shade of brown; woven straw shoes with ties up to knees; flax hair; rope over shoulder and around waist which ends in a peg; this boy also has another stick with a "golf-tee" type end; carries black rope in his hand; light brown checked pants; possibility that he was made before the Communist Revolution or perhaps the tag is just lacking the word "Soviet". Both boys are much alike, but there are some minor differences. *Shirley Karaba Collection.*

MARKS: "Willage Boy//Made in Russia" cotton tag.

SEE: *Illustration 200,* page 131. *Shirley Karaba Collection.*

Kirowz Man (Doll on left): 7in (18cm); cloth doll; eyebrows on diagonal line; heavy red cotton coat; red multi-colored belt; unusual pointed beige hat; wooden boots; 1930s.

MARKS: "Made in Soviet Union// 8096 H Kirowz" on edge of trousers.

Mordwa Woman (Doll on right): 8in (20cm); stuffed cloth body; stockinette head; gray felt coat trimmed with white tape; red stiffened cloth head-piece with red scarf wrapped around neck; red belt; white dress with red tape around hem; knapsack on back; straw shoes with leg straps; 1930s.

MARKS: "Made in Soviet//Mordwa" cloth tag on skirt.

SEE: *Illustration 201,* page 131. *Shirley Karaba Collection.*

Russian Peasant Woman: 9in (23cm); composition; picture shown in Romanian section.

White shawl covering head; red bolero trimmed with black fur; embroidered yellow bod-ice; blue skirt with white polka dots; carries basket on arms; before 1911.

MARKS: None.

SEE: *Illustration 186,* page 122. *McMasters Productions.*

Scotland

Scotland is part of Great Britain, however, the people have strong feelings about their independence. They have a different government and educational system

Scotland is now divided into regions; Dumfries and Galloway, the Borders, Strathclyde, Lothian, Central, Fife, Tayside, Grampian, Highland, Western Isles, Orkney and Shetland. They call their counties "shires" such as Argyll, Aberdeen, etc.

Most of their costumes center around plaid patterns. A plaid is a type of woolen cloth woven in stripes of various colors crossing at right angles so as to form a rectangular pattern. In order to get the exact pattern a piece of wood or pattern stick was wrapped with the exact number and color of threads to be used.

The original tartans probably represented districts rather than clans, but there are now clan and military plaids.

However, the people of Scotland also wore other clothes and dolls representing Scotland sometimes displayed these other fashions (see *Illustrations 205*, page 134 *and 207*, page 133.)

Scottish dolls at Sterling Castle.
(Dolls from left to right).
Bagpiper Made by Ilse Ludeke of Germany: 13in (33cm); all cloth; painted face; Steiff look-alike; seam down the center of face; red, green, white plaid pleated kilt; red felt coat; matching plaid scarf; lace jabot; coat trimmed with gold braid and sequins; real leather boots; fur sporron; well-made bagpipe; Scottish hat has gold button fastening a feather to it; 1970s.
MARKS: "Ilse Ludeke" on bottom of stand.
Liberty of London Scottish Man: 9in (23cm); soft sculpture face; cloth body; red hair; orange, green, white and black plaid skirt and scarf; black velvet jacket and tam; matching stockings; black beret; 1952-1953.
MARKS: "Liberty of London" cloth tag sewn in clothing.
Scottish Soldier Playing Bagpipe: 7in (18cm); bearskin fur hat of the Scottish Guards; tartan skirt and scarf; black belt jacket; lace jabot and cuffs; plaid trim around white boots; 1950s.
MARKS: "Liberty of London" cloth tag on clothes.
Mechanical Key Wind Scotsman: 9in (23cm); papier mâché socket head; cardboard body with mechanism inside; wood painted feet; red, white, black plaid kilt; matching tam; blue felt coat; white cloth sporron; key wind in back; 1930s.
MARKS: "Germany" printed on body.
SEE: *Illustration 206*, page 132.

(Dolls from left to right).

Scottish Man: 8in (20cm); velvet face and black coat; plaid wool bell-bottom pants; coat and pants are part of body construction; painted character face with one eye winking; open mouth with painted teeth; painted hair; applied single felt ears; 1930s.

MARKS: "Farnell//Alpha Toy Co.//Made in England" tag on left foot.

Herm Steiner Scottish Girl: 5in (13cm) bisque face; sleep eyes; open mouth; fully-jointed composition body; mohair wig; velvet Scottish hat with plaid trim and feather in back; black velvet coat; white blouse with gold buttons; blue, red and white plaid scarf, kilt, knee socks; painted shoes; fur sporron; original clothes; 1921+

MARKS: "Made in Germany//Herm Steiner" on back of head.

Hewitt and Leadbeater (Willow Pottery) Scottish Man: 10in (25cm); rough English white pottery head, arms, legs; molded hair; dressed in kilt with scarf of dark blue plaid with red and white stripes; silver pin with green jewel fastening the scarf to the black velvet coat; white shirt; sporron at waist with silver medallion; molded bisque legs to knees; white leggings with black buttons; 1918.

The bisque head was stuffed with a piece of newspaper which had a 1918 date on it and told how World War I was progressing.

Hewitt and Leadbeater were a Staffordshire pottery company. They were one of the first to make dolls during the war when England could no longer import German dolls for the children.

MARKS: None.

Scottish Lady in Green: 7in (18cm); all vinyl; blonde hair; dressed in bluish-green jumper-type dress trimmed in lace; blue and green plaid shawl; 1970s.

This unusual doll was purchased in a small castle where the "Lord of the Castle" was the tour guide. He said, "I wanted to show people that the 'ladies of yore' wore beautiful clothes - not just kilts."

MARKS: None.

SEE: *Illustration 207*, page 133.

Barleycorn Scottish Doll: 12.5in (32cm); cloth; 1975.

The Design Center of London is a showplace for English crafts. It displays and sells crafts made by British artists. There is always a good selection of artist dolls. In 1975 Thelma Purvis purchased this "Ancient Treasure" there.

MARKS: "Barleycorn//Design Center of London" on box.

SEE: *Illustration 204,* page 134. *Thelma Purvis Collection.*

Old Cottage Scottish Soldier: For information see *Illustration 37,* page 30.

Sheena Macleod Scottish Fishwife of 1845: 8in (20cm); sculpted, baked clay face and hands; cloth body over wire armature; black and white dress under gray and white striped homespun overskirt; bright red hand-knit sweater and large black shawl over her head; cloth cap under shawl; 1970s.

The doll is sitting on a cork base bending over a rope basket filled with real shells representing the day's catch.

Sheena Macleod is a well-known sculptor and doll maker. Each doll is different and interesting. Kimport imported a few of her dolls.

They included:

1. A **Crofter** seated on a wooden stump with his partially finished basket.

2. **Woman of the Isle of Skye** carrying a wicker basket filled with seaweed for her farmer husband to fertilize the crop.

3. **Shetland Knitting Woman** in authentic costuming.

4. **Easter Ross Fishwife** wearing a leather apron, woolen sweater, print scarf, and striped skirt; she holds before her a long shallow woven basket containing fishing lines that she is straightening for her husband. The long lines will be baited with cockles and mussels that she has collected from the rocks at low tide.

5. **New Haven Fish Wife on Gala Day.** The ladies of the city have a special dress for the Gala Day that shows the influence of the Dutch who used to cross the North Sea to fish for herring in the North of Scotland.

MARKS: None on doll.

SEE: *Illustration 205,* page 134.

Spain

Spain is a diverse land of strong emotions. Its government and boundaries have changed many times. A unifying force of the people has been their love of music, color, art and a historical desire to preserve the varying costumes through dolls. It is not an easy task to document all of the dolls when you realize that Spain is the third largest land mass in Europe (if you include the Balearic and Canary islands) after Russia and France.

Spanish doll collectors also should understand that many individual cities and villages within each area have their own special costumes which are similar but different in details. Even though many of their dolls are marked, it is often difficult to trace their regional identity.

Male Spanish Dancer with Castanets: 9in (23cm); Lenci Mascotte-type smooth linen-like painted face; gray felt bolero suit with black felt buttons and trim; handsome brown cobbled shoes; wooden castanets tied to wrists; maroon cummerbund; thread wig; ear in a single piece of gathered felt; circa 1930s.

This doll is from Andalusia and is a Flamingo dancer.

MARKS: None on doll; "N.A.T.I. Madrid//Lema//Novedad//Arte//Made in Spain" on box.

SEE: *Illustration 218*, page 135.

The Novedad Arte Tomalidad Ingenio Co. made dolls in many different sizes. The cloth dolls were made from linen-like material. An example of a doll from the region of Abulenses can be found on page 185 of the *Cloth Dolls Book* by the same authors. She is called *Girl in the Gold Dress*.

Canary Island Dancing Couple: 7in (18cm) vinyl head; felt hands, and body over wire armature; matching costumes.

Girl has white blouse, striped skirt, straw hat with streamers; black felt apron trimmed with red felt; blue earrings.

Boy has striped pants; white shirt; black felt jacket; red cummerbund and Spanish silk hat.

The Canary islands are an Atlantic Ocean winter vacation archipelago for both Europeans and Americans. There are seven of these Spanish Islands.

MARKS: "Bieler//Barcelona" on tag. The girl has the same tag with "Canaria" printed on it.

SEE: *Illustration 226*, page 135. *Louise Schnell Collection.*

Spanish Marriage Contract with Bride, Groom and Witness: 10in (25cm), 11in (28cm), 12in (31cm); each doll is fine quality linen over wax detailed character faces with glass eyes; molded eyelids; single stroke brows; two have closed mouths and the witness has an open/closed mouth with teeth; original hair; unjointed bodies with good detail; wax fingers individually wrapped with linen.

Original clothing with fine lace, embroidery, and other details. The stitching on the costumes is all done by hand.

The witness (possibly a duena) holds a book which records the marriage contract.

The translation says: "Marriage declaration made in the village of S. Joaquin in 1842 Vwlonfinf to Natmalee that we will announce ahead in the department of Nefuo the 19th day of the month of August 1842."

Due to the condition of the document, this was a difficult translation.

This is a rare example of early Spanish clothing.

SEE: *Illustration 208,* page 136. *McMaster Productions.*

Spanish Googly Lenci: 20in (51cm); all felt body; glass "flirty" eyes; painted face; black mohair hair; large open mouth; individual fingers (rare for Lenci); black taffeta dress with orange felt circles and trim; large felt roses and green leaves at waist line; large gold earrings and gold necklace; 6in (15cm) red wooden comb with second group of roses near hair; beautiful lace mantilla covers comb; Spanish-type ruffles at bottom of skirt; ruffled petticoat and teddy; felt shoes; lace gloves. This is a hard-to-find Lenci version of the *Widow* dressed in an Andulucian costume; 1920s.

MARKS: None.

SEE: *Illustration 209,* page 136 and front cover.

Granada is a mecca for tourists to Andalusia because of the Alhambra of "Arabian Nights" fame. Here the Moors made their last stand in Spain. The Alhambra is the entire complex on the hilltop in the city of Granada. It includes a business section as well as the beautifully restored Alcazaba Fortress. It is also a center of Spanish gypsies and their flamingo dancing. The picture in the background of *Illustration 214* shows a famous scene in one of the gardens of the Alcazaba.

Spanish Flamingo Male Dancer (Doll on left): 5in (13cm); cloth face; cloth over armature body; dances with the help of a circular wire attached to his feet; 1964.

MARKS: None.

Flamingo Dancer (Doll on right): 11in (28cm); cloth painted face, blue plastic Spanish high comb and earrings; cloth over armature body; red and white polka dot cotton dress with ribbon trim; yellow shawl with long fringe; mohair wig; holding castanets; bracelet on right arm; 1970s.

MARKS: "Layna" made in Spain.

SEE: *Illustration 214, page 137.*

TALLERES ARTE FUSTE (T.A.F.)

In 1934 a doll company in Madrid put out a catalog with sepia pictures of their 1934 line. It was a beautiful catalog featuring dolls modelled after Lenci and other Italian dolls. However, these dolls had their own Spanish "flavor". The costumes were well designed and made. They could compete on the world market with some of the most expensive cloth dolls made during that period.

They are not well known in the United States, and the few that have been found were in the Southwestern states where there is a large Spanish population.

The company not only made regional dolls, but their line included a series of little girl dolls, and dolls that play with toys, hoops, spinning wands, jump ropes, etc.

A sports and party series for both girls and boys included golfers, sailors, walkers, cowboys, swimmers, and dolls dressed for parties.

Teen age dolls included regional and party dolls. One special doll was dressed as a Spanish priest.

A series of women tourist dolls represented the adult dancers from various provinces.

There were also speciality dolls. One 13.5in (34cm) doll came inside a beautifully decorated Easter egg.

Their "Municas Humoristicas Line" competed with Nistis and Klumpe dolls.

The "Art Deco" boudoir dolls were listed as Munecas Decoratives, wearing lavish costumes.

The dolls of the 1930s regions can be seen in *Illustrations 210-213, page 138-139.* Some of the regions have changed names, but it is possible to identify pre-World War II Spanish dolls with these pictures.

Today some of the regions have similar names, but most have been conquered and consolidated. The new regions are:

1. Along the Mediterranean Coast: Catalonia.
2. Northeast: Aragon.
3. North Central: Navarre, Asturias.
4. Northwest: Galicia.
5. North Central (from east to west): Castile, Leon.
6. East Central: Valencia.
7. Central: Castile, Leon, Extremadura.
8. South East: Murcia.
9. South: Andalusia.

Old Castile is comprised of the old provinces of Vallidod, Segovia, Avila, Burgos, LaGrono, Palencia, Soria, Salamanca and La Mora.

The provinces were conquered, or joined forces with others. The boundaries were blurred. For the doll collector this makes identification difficult.

Some of the provinces shown in the T.A.F. catalog can no longer be found on maps or

in *Travelers Guides.* Legarteros is now only shown as a lace making area. Vizcainos is part of the Basque Country in the North. Ronda, along the Andulusian Coast (a unique area), and Charros seems to have disappeared or been swallowed up by new boundaries.

But the purpose of this book is to try to keep a historical record of the regional dolls and a list of the companies which made the dolls. If you have any information about the history of these dolls, please send it to the authors in care of Hobby House Press.

Gallegos Boy: 14in (36cm) very firm body; stiffened fine muslin; painted eyelashes above eyes; light eyebrows; bow mouth with cloudy white dot in center; applied ears; black plush wig; neat hand-sewn seam in head; no side seams; jointed at shoulders and hips only; arms operate together when moved; unusual widely-spaced fingers with second and third fingers indicated only by stitching; little finger and thumb more pointed than fingers of other cloth dolls; body and limbs of fine, woven muslin; dressed in Gallegos musician's costume; white muslin shirt with cuffs open; front of vest is maroon felt with white felt in back; black felt knee-length pants with white cloth inset at hem; black high felt boots with felt buttons; blue cotton cummerbund; brown felt provincial hat with black felt brim and pompons; 1934.

The catalog shows the boy carrying a bagpipe. This boy is from the Galicia province of northwest Spain. The population traces its roots to the Celts, and bagpipes are a common musical instrument. Galicia is a poor agricultural region which is heavily populated. The climate is different from the rest of Spain because it gets more rain. However, over the years, the land has been divided into very tiny impoverished farms.

MARKS: "Talleres De Arte//Fuste//Impuesto De Lujo Ametalico//Permiso No. 359 Factura No. 1107" (sticker on bottom of left foot).

SEE: *Illustration 210,* page 138.

Talleres De Arte Fuste (T.A.F.) Workshops of the Art of Fueste Munecas Regionales (Regions) 1 & 2 Catalanes; 3 & 4 Valencianos; 5 & 6 Andaluces; 7 & 8 Charros.

Catalanes: From the Catalonia Province along the Pyrenees in northwest Spain.

Valencianos: From the province of Valencia in southwest Spain.

Andaluces: From the province of Andalucia in southeast Spain.

Charros: Peasants from Salamanca in Castile in central Spain.

SEE: *Illustration 211*, page 139.

9 & 10 Alcarrenos; 11 & 12 Vizcainos; 13 & 14 Aragoness; 15 & 16 Legarteranos.

Alcarrenos: From Cuenca Province which is southeast of Madrid

Vizcainos: From Vizcaya. This is Basque country around the Biscay Bay in Northern Spain.

Legarteranos: Wine pressers from the Toledo area in La Mancha - now Old Castile.

Aragoneses: From the Aragon province in the Pyrenees section of northern Spain.

SEE: *Illustration 212*, page 139.

17 & 18 Castelianos; 19 & 20 Rondenos; 21 & 22 Abulenses; 23 & 24 Gallegos.

Castelianos: From the provinces of Old and New Castile.

Rondenos: From Rondo in the province of Andalusia.

Abulenses: From Albacete in La Mancha. It is famous for saffron.

Gallegos: From the province of Galicia; see *Illustration 210*, page 138.

SEE: *Illustration 213*, page 139.

Gypsy Playing a Violin: 10in (25cm); carved wood; painted face and hair; yellow taffeta shirt; orange bolero with green rickrack and felt flowers; black velvet pants; large real leather shoes; green ribbon turban.

Many Spanish gypsies live in caves in the Sacromonte hills near Granada in the province of Andolucia.
MARKS: "A Paquita Doll Figurine// Gypsy created by Paquita" tag on doll.
SEE: *Illustration 215,* page 140.

Catalonian Man with Walking Stick (Doll on left): 7in (18cm); hard vinyl face; felt body over armature; black velvet suit; red ribbon belt; brown sandals; late 1960s.

Walking is a favorite activity in the Pyrenees mountains. There are many paths with wonderful views. Since Catalonia is a province that borders France, hiking into the Catalon section of the Pyrenees mountains in France is a popular avocation. Citizens of both countries dance the Sardane at similar festivals (see *Illustrations 60-61,* page 44, 45..)
MARKS: "Bielier//Barcelona" on gold tag; "Catalan" paper label pinned on suit.
Girl from Segovia with Walking Stick: 6.5in (17cm); hard vinyl face; felt over armature; red cotton skirt; black felt top; lace scarf; triangular felt hat with pom poms at each point; felt walking shoes; gold walking stick; late 1960s.

Marin made a doll with a similar Segovia costume holding a flute instead of a walking stick.
MARKS: "Segoviana" white tag pinned on doll. The company is Bieler.
SEE: *Illustration 216,* page 140. *Louise Schnell Collection.*

Matador (Doll on left):
12in (31cm); all hard plastic; green, flirty eyes; stiffened pink taffeta jacket, bolero, and pants; gold trim down arms and legs; gold tassles at knees; socket head; heavy black wool stiffened hat; 1950s.

Ferdinand the Bull by Ideal of the United States (on right): 10in (25cm) long; all composition; 1939.

MARKS: None on Matador; "Ideal Novelty & Toy Co.//Made in U.S.A. © Dent" on bull.

SEE: *Illustration 217, page 141. Sandra Strater Collection.*

Doll from Lagerterana (Doll on left): 7in (18cm); unusual, waxy vinyl face; cloth body on armature; beautifully painted face; black shawl trimmed with gold ornaments; black bodice with gold braid; red cotton skirt with colorful ribbon trim at hem; black apron with similar ribbon trim; white kerchief; legs painted to imitate colorful knitted stockings; early 1970s.

Lagerterana is a town in the province of Valencia. The doll is very different from the normal dolls of this province. These localized costumes can be found throughout Europe.

MARKS: "Muneca Artesana//Beibi//Autentico Rraje Regional//Made in Spain" on base; "Valenciano" also found on base.

Girl from Badajoz: 11in (28cm); molded cloth face; cloth body on armature; lovely painted face; black cotton blouse; yellow skirt; white taffeta apron with ribbon stripes; white color trimmed with lace; flannel shoes with ties to her knees.

Badajoz is one of the two divisions of the province of Extredura which borders Portugal. The other division is Caceres. This little-visited province is called the "Cradle of the Conquistadors."

They claim the explorers Cortes, Pizarro, Balboa, De Sota, and many others. The roots of the people are in the soil.

MARKS: "G. Marcade Garanta//Artesan//Espanol" tag. "Badajoz" back of tag.

SEE: *Illustration 222, page 141.*

Humorous Dolls: Klumpe, Nistis, T.A.F. and other Spanish companies developed a "cartoonish-type" of doll that has become very collectible in the United States and Europe. They are well-made and fun to have displayed around a house. People who do not collect dolls enjoy the humor in their unusual poses. It is much like laughing at the cartoons or "funny pages" of our childhood. Prices of these dolls have dramatically risen in the last several years.

There are hundreds of different dolls from various companies. Other Spanish companies also make them.

Matador and Bull: *Bull* is 7in (18cm) long and 4.5in (12cm) tall; *Matador* is 7in (18cm) tall; bull is made from black plush material; head of matador is stiffened cloth head; felt over armature body; white satin matador suit with pink metallic trim; hat made of looped thread; face painted in Klumpe fashion with inverted "V" eyebrows; red felt cape with yellow lining; bull has two picks in his body with red yarn imitating blood; 1960s-1970s.
MARKS: "Klumpe//N. io-ME//Made in Spain" tag on doll.
SEE: *Illustration 219*, page 142.

Andalusian Dancer: 30in (76cm); composition shoulder plate head; felt body with long torso; ladies' figure; embroidered hair with "spit" curls of the period; red organdy dress with black felt trim; pom poms made of net covering body and comb in hair; cobbled shoes; 1930s.
MARKS: None.
SEE: *Illustration 220*, page 142. *Joseph Golembieski Collection.*

Girl in Spanish Cowgirl Suit (Doll on left): 11.75in (30cm); polished cotton face; cloth over armature body; real leather Spanish riding outfit complete with lariat and Spanish riding hat. Spain has always been a country devoted to horses; dolls with riding outfits are found in many of the provinces.

Girl with Straw Hat (Doll on right): 10.5in (27cm); polished cotton face; cloth over armature body; striped skirt; blue and white striped apron; white shawl with lace trim under straw hat; carries basket of oranges. Her provincial costume is probably from Valencia.

MARKS: "Munecas//Layna// Made in Spain" on tag.
SEE: *Illustration 227, page 143. Shirley Karaba Collection.*

Segoviano Man (Doll on left): 8in (20cm); finely sculptured vinyl head, hands, and body; excellently costumed man with black cape; knee length pants, vest with six buttons; undervest trimmed in gold; white shirt; Spanish-type hat; red cummerbund-type belt with gold chain; walking stick; all original; 1970s.

The Marin Company is a modern company which makes dolls that are beautifully costumed. Along with their regional lines, they make beautiful historical dolls, especially of royalty.

Segovia is northwest of Madrid in the Old Castile.
MARKS: "Marin//Chiclana// Espana//Segovianna" on man's tag.

Segoviano Woman (Doll on right): finely sculpted vinyl head, hands, and body; red skirt with blue and gold embroidery; black blouse; lace scarf; black apron, matching headpiece with red and yellow pom poms; woman carries a flute; all original; 1970s. Many of the faces of the dolls of Jose Marin Verdugo have been inspired by Sophia Loren, as is this one.

The Marin boxes are beautifully decorated with pretty flowers. This box is marked "Joven Segoviana."
MARKS: "Marin//Chiclana//Espana// Segovianna" on tag.

SEE: *Illustration 224, page 143. Louise Schnell Collection.*

Gaucho-type Boy from Zamorano (Doll on left): 13in (33cm); all cloth doll; well-painted face; separate sewn-on ear gathered to look like a

cup; double chin; black suit is a heavy faille-type material with double set of gold buttons; felt hat; white shirt; red cummerbund; serape draped over right shoulder; leather boots; 1920s-1930s.

Zamorano is in the western part of the Old Castile. This is not too far from Madrid.

MARKS: "Zamorano R P//27/46// Made in Spain" blue and white sticker on bottom of shoe.

Girl from Zamorano (Doll on right): 13in (33cm); all cloth doll; well-painted face with heavy gray eye shadow; eyelashes different from the boy; eyebrows are slit which causes a ridge under the eye and then painted black; double chin; fine thread hair for wig; flowered print dress with three ruffles on skirt; black trim on ruffles and sleeves; white blouse; white scarf with angora-like blue fringe; no ears, but has gold earrings; holds castanets decorated with pom poms; hair is in knot in back; blue shoes.

Zamorano is in the western part of the Old Castile.

MARKS: None.

SEE: *Illustration 223*, page 144. *Nancy Bakes Collection.*

Spanish Lady (Doll on left): 15in (38cm); celluloid head; cloth hands and body; painted face; mohair wig with pearls entwined in hair; cream batiste dress with ruffles on sleeves and skirt; pink pom pom at neckline; gold bracelet with coin; 1930s. The style of the dress is centuries older.

This doll's costume is the type of dress worn in Madrid when wealthy ladies were joining their husbands to populate the various South and Central American countries. The dress is very similar to the national costume of Panama.

MARKS: "Kersa" on back of doll's head.

Girl in Gold Dress (Doll on right): 13in (33cm); molded cotton painted face, heavy, raised eyebrows; heavy eye shadow; blonde floss braided hair entwined with hair; Spanish comb in back of head; papier mâché body jointed with newsprint; cloth legs; gold tapestry dress; black ribbon belt; white net apron.

MARKS: "Made in Madrid."

SEE: *Illustration 225*, page 144. *Shirley Karaba Collection.*

Sweden

Sweden is the largest of the Scandinavian countries containing a history of the Vikings.

The people are very interested in retaining their provincial costumes, dances, music, houses, etc. (see *Illustration 230,* page 145.)

Swedish costumes, while very colorful, are plainer than those of Denmark and Norway. The skirts of the women are shorter to allow greater movement in their dances. Usually there is a bodice or corselet laced up in the front and worn over a white blouse. It is often laced with silver or pewter. Each region has its own variation either in the apron or dress. Shawls are very popular. To help with the problem of no pockets, many of the costumes have a flat square or oval embroidered bag suspended from the waistband with colored braids.

The men's costumes favor yellow or blue (see *Illustration 234,* page 147.)

Swedish Provinces
1. Blekinge
2. Dalarna
3. Halland
4. Häverö
5. Helsingland Region
6. Insjon
7. Leksand
8. Rättavik
9. Smaland
10. Soldermanland
11. Vanga

12. Varmland
13. Skane
14. Gotland is an island.
15. Oland is an island.

Charlotte Weibull

A short hydrofoil ride across the choppy North Sea from Copenhagen, Denmark, is the town of Malmo, Sweden. Disembarking, the visitor will see a charming "Old World" square called Lilla Torg. This is the home of a half-timbered building pictured in the background of *Illustration 230,* page 145. where a multitude of charming Swedish dolls can be seen and purchased.

Charlotte Weibull is known as "the keeper of the traditional costumes and lore of Sweden." She not only makes dolls, but she also makes the costumes for various folk festivities. A few of these costumes can be seen in the background where a dance festival for all ages was being held the day when Polly and Pam visited (and bought) the dolls.

Charlotte Weibull has made dolls for many years, and the variety is infinite. Each doll is made with care and usually boxed with an explanation of the lore surrounding it.

Bride from Osterlen (Doll on left): 7in (18cm) stockinette head and body; painted face; wooden shoes.

According to the brochure in the box, "On the eve of the wedding one of the bridesmaids came to the home of the bride to help her dress, a procedure that lasted the whole night through. While she was being dressed the bride stood and wore a coin in each shoe. This was supposed to bring her happiness and good fortune in her new home.

"Slowly she was dressed in her complete bridal outfit, the lace-embellished chemise, the pleated skirt, the pearl-embroidered bodice, the silken-edged jacket, and the white linen apron.

"The apron string (seen on the doll's right) was covered by a ribbon which had a beautiful pattern in red and white and sent around the bride's waist as many times as the number of chests she had in her dowry.

"The red bridal ribbons (pieces of felt) on the left were adorned with gold and silver lace and the bride's name embroidered in silk. These were so wide that the apron could barely be seen underneath. The richer the bride, the wider the ribbons.

"The jacket had a low neck so that the pearl-embroidered bodice could be seen. Tucked into this bodice were two small silver spoons to be used at the wedding feast.

"Handkerchief, knitted gloves and a hymn book were also part of the wedding outfit.

"The bride wore much jewelry, the most beautiful of all being the cross given to her by her bridegroom the day she consented to marry him. The red headdress was also adorned with gold and silver lace and had silk ribbons hanging at the back. The bride's hair hung loose, and last of all the headdress was placed upon her head. When the time came for the bride to thank her fiddler, she took one of the ribbons off her headdress and fastened it to his violin.

"Then the mother-in-law had to cut the bride's long hair and put a white coif on her head. Thus, her hair was completely covered because as a married woman, she was no longer allowed to be attractive to other men."

MARKS: "CHARLOTTE WEIBULL//AKARP SWEDEN" seal on plastic box.

Peasant Doll (Doll in middle): 6in (15cm); stockinette face; wooden peg body; thread hair; printed striped skirt; holding feathers.

This is an inexpensive doll made so that almost every child (or doll collector) could afford to take one home.

MARKS: "CHARLOTTE WEIBULL//AKARP SWEDEN" seal on plastic box.

Tailor (Doll on right): 8in (20cm) seated on table; stockinette body; gray wool suit; striped shirt. He is shown with a needle through the material. On the table is a pincushion with pins and scissors.

MARKS: "Charlotte Weibull//Akarp Sweden" seal on box.

SEE: *Illustration 230,* page 145.

This is a Swedish classroom created by Charlotte Weibull representing the early part of this century. It is a type of one-room school, and each child has a different assignment in his or her book. Some draw, others print, still others read a hard assignment. Each child has a different face. Some are serious. Some are mischievous. The boy in the middle of the first row is trying to kick the boy next to him.

There are six girls and three boys. All have blonde hair. Each costume is different. Some children have wooden shoes. Others have leather ones.

The teachers carry a "stick", and their expression indicates they use it upon occasion. There is a Scandinavian map on the front of each teacher's desk.

Teachers: 8in (20cm); **Children:** 5in (13cm); cloth over wire armature so dolls can be "positioned"; 1970s.

MARKS: None on dolls.

SEE: *Illustration 231,* page 145.

Sveg Girl (Doll on left):
5in (13cm); modern composition; black cap over lace cap; white blouse; brown scarf with fringe; brown skirt with lines painted on dress; brown pouch hanging with design painted on it; 1993.

MARKS: "Handverk" on blue seal with yellow cross painted on base. "Made in Sweden" seal on plastic container.

Viking (Doll in middle): 5in (13cm); modern composition; brown Viking tunic; black Viking hat with horns; brown and tan shield; painted shoes, stockings, and ties; 1993.

MARKS: "Dockan//Made in Sweden// Handverk" on seal on base.

Oland Girl (Doll on right): 5in (13cm); modern composition head and body; painted face; white kerchief on head; white blouse with double collar trimmed with lace; silver brooch; black weskit; yellow skirt with brown bias trim; red apron with painted embroidery around hem; painted stockings and shoes; 1993.

MARKS: "Handverk" on blue seal with yellow cross on it on base; "Made in Sweden" seal on container.

SEE: *Illustration 228,* page 147.

These are well-made dolls for their size.

Skane Boy with Wooden Fiddle or Violin: 7in (18cm) painted knit face; cotton body; yellow knit pants with yarn around hem; black felt vest with red trim; white shirt with red and white embroidered trim; leather shoes; 1970s.

MARKS: "Charlotte Weibull" on tag.

SEE: *Illustration 234,* page 147. *Louise Schnell Collection.*

Peddler from Blekinge: 8in (20cm); stockinette painted face; gray mohair wig and whiskers; stockinette body; brown wool overcoat; gray wool pants; black felt leg warmers with buttons around bottom of legs; black wooden shoes; striped wool vest; white shirt; high black felt hat; 1970s.

He is selling raw wool and wool material; carries walking stick with bell on it.
MARKS: "Charlotte Weibull" tag on doll.
SEE: *Illustration 232, page 148.*

Sailor from the Ship, the Gripsholm, at Gripsholm Castle: 13in (33cm); blue uniform forms the body; smiling sculptured face; double seamed ears; side-glancing eyes with one white dot; painted reddish brown hair; blue felt uniform with yellow felt trim and brass buttons; matching sailor cap with *Gripsholm* embroidered on it in yellow; felt hands which are wired to hold bouquet of flowers. A tag with flowers says, "With compliments//Swedish-American Line."

Gripsholm Castle, a 16th century castle is three and a half hours by steamer on Lake Malar from Stockholm.

Norah Wellings made many sailor dolls which were sold aboard ships. The ship the *Gripsholm* was commissioned in 1924. During World War II it served as a peace ship exchanging diplomatic representatives of warring countries.

MARKS: None on doll. However, it was made by Norah Wellings.
SEE: *Illustration 233, page 148.*

Leksand Dalarna Region Man and Woman: 5in (13cm) each; clay head; wire armature body; mohair wig.
Man (Doll on left): Yellow knickers with red pom poms hanging down from the bottom of pants; blue coat with red trim; simulated red and yellow embroidery; black felt hat trimmed in red.
Woman (Doll on right): black skirt, red apron with black, green, white stripes; red vest with black and yellow stripes; white blouse and organdy neckerchief and cap; white and red print sash; 1993.
MARKS: "DOKANA" on tag.
SEE: *Illustration 229, page 149. Barbara Comienski Collection. James Comienski photographer.*

Switzerland

Switzerland is a small, mountainous country in the heart of Europe. It is about half the size of Maine and bordered by four countries: Germany on the north; Italy on the south; France on the west; Liechtenstein and Austria on the east.

With so many countries nearby, a long tradition of neutrality and a haven for people fleeing from their own country, Switzerland shares many languages. German, French and Italian are their three official languages, but an unofficial one is the ancient spoken Roman especially in Graubunden in the East.

Their costumes naturally reflect the costumes of the countries whose language they speak.

Years ago we read that old Swiss people wore real silver with most of their old costumes. They also used genuine silver on their old dolls in past times. If the reader has an old Swiss doll with silver chains, look for the silver mark. We did on the doll in *Illustration 238*, page 152 and found the mark. We were delighted.

The Provinces of Switzerland are called Cantons:

1. Aargau
2. Appenzell-Ausserrhoden*
3. Appenzell-Innerrhoden*
4. Basel-Lands*
5. Basel-Stadt*
6. Bern (Berne)
7. Fribourg (Freiburg)
8. Geneva (Gef)
9. Glarus (Glaris)
10. Graubunder (Grisons)
11. Jura
12. Luzern (Lucerne)
13. Neuchatle (Neuenburg)
14. Nidwalden*
15. Obwalden*
16. St. Gallen (St. Gall)
17. Schaffhausen (Schaffhouse)
18. Schwyz
19. Solothurn (Soleure)
20. Thurgau (Thurgovie)
21. Ticino (Tessin)
22. Uri

23. Vallais (Wallis)
24. Zug (Zoug)
25. Zurich

*Half cantons.

These cantons are listed in case the reader has a doll with a provincial tag. This is the way we identified some of our dolls. Other dolls have tags with the name of the Swiss city.

Sheepherder: 11.5in (29cm); clay Santon-type doll; made by doll artist Claude Carbonet; striped shirt; felt vest; long cloak with hood covering rest of clothing; carrying sheep in left hand; staff in right hand; 1958.
MARKS: None.
SEE: *Illustration 235,* page 150. *Thelma Purvis Collection.*

Joanna from Lugano: 12in (31cm); all celluloid; blue felt jacket; grey skirt; white and red apron; red close-fitting cap; large earrings; wearing a cross necklace; 1955.
MARKS: "Joanna//Lugano//Made in Switzerland" on wrist tag.
SEE: *Illustration 236.,* page 150.

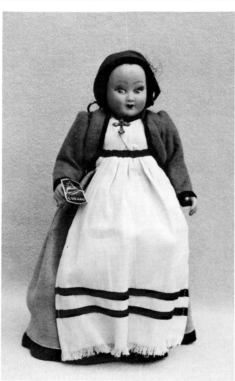

Sometime in the 1960s or 1970s a company made a line of provincial doll house dolls. They came in pretty orange boxes lined on the inside with paper lace. The name of the country was stamped on the inside bottom of the box. The name of the company was not on the box. These dolls are very well made for their size. This picture shows the *Swiss Pair, Illustration 244,* page 151. The German section pictures the doll from Helgoland. These are nice additions to an International collection, and they do not take up much space to store.
Man (Doll on left): 4in (10cm); German composition; jointed at shoulders and hips; molded painted face; beige felt coat and knee breeches (almost like a *Mozart-type* costume; red felt vest; white shirt; black felt tricorner hat and bow tie.
MARKS: "Germany" stamped on foot. "Switzerland" stamped in purple inside the box.
Woman (Doll on right): 3.5in (9cm); German composition; jointed at shoulders and hips; black felt bonnet (not as pointed as it looks); white blouse; black felt "V" shaped weskit with yarn for ties; green cotton skirt; orange apron with orange and green tulips printed on it. This costume looks very similar to the one from Schaffhausen Canton.
MARKS: "Germany" stamped on foot. "Swiss" stamped in purple inside the box.
SEE: *Illustration 244,* page 151.

Bern (Doll on left): 13in (33cm); bisque shoulderhead; white kid body; blonde mohair wig in braids; sleep eyes; feathered brows; open mouth with four teeth; velvet weskit is hand-beaded; quantity of silver chains; silver floral stud buttons; sateen shirt; velvet ribbon and lace head-dress; heavy cotton blouse with black lace at bottom of sleeve; space between neck closing and top of weskit; came with original box.

MARKS: "A. & M." on back of head; "K & K" on box.

Bern (Doll on right): 8in (20cm); bisque head; open mouth with four teeth; sleep eyes; single stroke eyebrows; mohair wig in bun; all jointed composition body with turned wrists; black weskit with space between neck closing and top of weskit; white organdy blouse; pale roses on light apron over red skirt; black lace hat with flowers; gold yarn closing weskit; gold hanging ribbon; 1924.

UNUSUAL IDENTIFICATION FEATURE FOR BERN COSTUME: Weskit has high neck clos-

ing with space before top of actual weskit. Also the headdress looks like "wings" of lace.

MARKS: "71//Unis//France//60//149//14/0" on back of head.

SEE: *Illustration 243*, page 151. *Shirley Karaba Collection.*

Ausser Rhoden Appenzell Little Boy (Doll on left): 10in (25cm); white linen shirt; black felt tie and suspenders with silver braids attached to pale yellow felt breeches; scarlet waistcoat with silver buttons; black felt trim at bottom of breeches with ribbon and silver buttons; black felt shoes; black felt hat; 1920s.

MARKS: None.

Ausser Rhoden Appenzell Little Girl (Doll on right): 10in (25cm); pressed cloth body; high-color face; painted eyes; marcelled, braided mohair wig tied with red ribbons; black and white wired net headdress with red rosettes on each side; red ribbon in back; white laced blouse with black bands at sleeves; black weskit laced with silver chains and silver buttons; silver braids holding chain over shoulders and down the front; inset of floral silk at top center of weskit; yellow insert in weskit matches yellow apron; finely pleated red skirt to make her look slim; black felt tie shoes; 1920s.

MARKS: None.

SEE: *Illustration 239, page 152. Sandra Strater Collection.*

Inner Rhoden Appenzell Married Lady: 10.5in (27cm); European composition; brown glass sleep eyes; mohair wig; closed mouth; socket head; fully jointed composition body; pleated bluish-green skirt with black bodice; white blouse with puffed sleeves trimmed with ribbon and lace; black weskit with silver chains; blue turned purple collar with lace and gold braid trim; matching apron; big butterfly headdress with lace trim (Schlappe); black ribbon in back; finely pleated skirt to make her look slim; many real silver chains with floral medallions; black patent leather shoes with silver buckles; 1930s.

Her costume indicates she is a married lady.

MARKS: "Made//in//Switzerland" black tag sewn on petticoat.

SEE: *Illustration 238, page 152.*

Girl from Vaud (Doll on left): 8.5in (22cm); European hard plastic; straw hat worn slanted; green ribbon hanging down; white blouse; white skirt with green ribbon trim; black vest with a red brooch; black apron with green ribbon trim; late 1950s-early 1960s.

The bridge is the famous covered bridge which crossed the river in Lucerne. It burned down in 1992.

MARKS: "Grivelli//souvenir//Vaud" round gold tag on doll.

Wachau Girl (Doll on right): This is an Austrian Doll from Niederosterreich which is in lower Austria. 7in (19cm); hard plastic head; vinyl hands and legs; cloth body; gold crocheted crown headdress; dark purple print taffeta dress with white collar trimmed with lace; silver brooch at neckline.; 1970s.

MARKS: "Feldkirch//Made in Austria" on tag with big flower.

SEE: *Illustration 240, page 153.*

Mountain Man: 7.5in (19cm); painted plaster-type head and hands; all metal, ballbearing, jointed metal body; soft cotton wrapped around body to make it realistic; legs covered with cardboard; jointed at head, wrists, elbows, shoulders, hips, knees, ankles; dressed in white shirt; black felt jacket with red trim; buttons down the front; yellow pants; white stockings; black metal feet.

All the metal joints "Pop" off like the modern Pop-it beads; heads can be interchanged and cos-tumes easily changed. There is a series of Swiss costumed dolls. There were also firemen, clowns, black men, Bescassine, rabbit, Mrs. Katzenjammer and Kids, baseball players, and others; patented in 1921.

Alpine Girl (Doll on right): 10in (25cm); all very heavy bisque; socket head; jointed at shoulders and hips; molded, painted hair and face; dressed in generic Alpine costume; white cotton blouse; cotton print apron and scarf with white, blue, lavender Alpine flowers; socks and shoes are painted bisque; carries straw basket with same colored flowers in it.

MARKS: "Double circle with arrow in middle" inscribed in bisque on back of neck.

SEE: *Illustration 237, page 154.*

Wales

Wales is located on the western part of the island of Great Britain. They were once an independent, vigorous country with their own language and customs. While today they are part of the English Empire, they work hard to retain their customs including language, writings, music and costumes. They continue to have festivals, especially musical ones.

They do have some differences in costumes, but the traditional woman's costume has the black "stovepipe-type" hat (see *Illustration 245, page 155.*); 1930s.

MARKS: None on doll; made by Bucherer of Switzerland.

SEE: *Illustrations 241, page 154 and 242, page 153.*

These are modern bisque dolls purchased in Lucerne, Switzerland in 1988.

St Bernard (Doll on left): 5in (13cm) high; 7in (18cm) long; nicely modeled dog.

MARKS: "AKITA" printed on one paw; "Vaga International" on another paw.

Alpine Boy (Doll in middle): 10in (25cm); same body characteristics as girl; white cotton shirt; brown velvet Alpine jacket with black tape trim; gray corduroy Alpine short pants; matching pointed Alpine hat.

MARKS: "Double circle with arrow in middle" inscribed in bisque on back of neck.

Traditional Welsh Woman's Costume: 8in (20cm); stiffened cloth mask; face sculptured with wide grin; cloth hands and legs; red velvet body and arms; blue, white, yellow plaid apron decorated with French knots; blue and white scarf; black felt "stovepipe" hat tied under the chin.

MARKS: "Made in England//by//Norah Wellings" tag sewn on bottom of left foot.

SEE: *Illustration 245, page 155.* This is a Norah Wellings doll.

Norah Wellings made this type of "tourist doll" featuring the costumes of many parts of the wide English Empire. These dolls were not only sold in Great Britain, but they could be found in shops in the various islands and other British "possessions" so they and their children could understand the people in other parts of their huge Empire.

Myfanwy (My Rare One): 7.5in (19cm); English hard plastic; red flannel skirt; white flannel top; painted black shoes; stovepipe hat with lace around bottom of hat; 1950s-1960s.

MARKS: "Sarold//Myfanwy (My Rare One)//Welsh Dressed Doll//Guaranteed Dressed in Genuine Welsh Flannel//Made in Wales" on box.

SEE: *Illustration 246., page 155. Ester Borgis Collection.*

Yugoslavia

Life has changed in this country since the fall of communism. Like the rest of the world, clothing has also changed to pants and tops for both men and women, as in the other parts of the world for everyday wear. However, the dolls in this section show the folkloric costumes of the area.

This is a land that is still caught between the European and Asiatic world. It is a land of conflicting customs, religions, and politics. Throughout the centuries these middle eastern countries have grouped and regrouped. These are the various areas of this once united Yugoslavia.

1. Slovenia
2. Croatia
3. Bosnia-Hercegovina
4. Serbia
5. Montenegro
6. Macedonia

Slovenian Couple: 15in (38cm) both dolls; all hand carved from wood; painted face; dolls are hand dressed in exquisite detail; woman has blue satin taffeta skirt; vest is dark blue cotton; hand embroidered brocade shawl with gold button; elaborate headdress is pink with gold braid; man wears tight black suede pants with black velvet embroidered vest; black cotton cape; cobbled boots are leather; carries red umbrella; black hat has red feather; 1970s.

The red umbrella seems traditional for the male Slovenian doll.
MARKS: None.
SEE: *Illustration 247*, page 156. *Kathy Lincoln Collection.*

Slovenian Girl from Ljubljana: 28in (71cm); all vinyl; sleep eyes; synthetic wig with braids; jointed at neck, shoulders, hips; individual fingers; beautiful white organdy over pink smocked high headdress worn only by married women; black velvet band on front of hat with gold and copper sequins edged in white lace over velvet; cream-colored blouse trimmed in lace; magenta scarf woven with multi-colored metallic thread; royal blue satin skirt; dark blue velvet band around bottom of skirt; black silk apron edged in black lace; gold chain down and around to edge of apron; red, white, blue ribbon bow on chain.

The chain holds the handkerchief which is part of the dance. Instead of holding hands as the partners dance, they pass the handkerchief back and forth. The ribbons on the chain are symbols of the Slovenian flag.

Unmarried girls wear the same costume, but they wear a scarf on their head.

This picture was taken in Annie's restaurant in Chesterland, Ohio. As diners come into the restaurant they see a very large painting of a Slovenian couple dancing the polka. They also see the doll with the same costume including the ribbon on the chain.

MARKS: None on doll.
SEE: *Illustration 248,* page 156. *Ana Leben Collection.*

Yugoslavian Couple (Dolls on left): 7.5in (19cm); both dolls have soft painted cloth faces; felt hands; body is wire armature. Man has blue velvet vest; short velvet pants; white pants show above leather boots; white blouse; orange scarf around shoulders under vest; black felt hat with green, white, pink, red felt trim. Woman dressed in white blouse with pleated sleeves; brown vest; white printed silk scarf; red ribbon belt; gold chain around waist; head has embroidered scarf tied in back; late 1950s.
MARKS: "Made in Yugoslavia" tag around man's leg.
Croation Lady (Doll in middle): 8in (20cm); cloth mask embroidered face; cloth over armature body; black thread hair wig; white blouse with trim; white apron with same trim; red polka dot sash and matching scarf; gray leather shoes with fancy embroidery; very well-made doll; 1958.
MARKS: "Hand Made in Yugoslavia//Original Costume as worn in Croatia//Made in Yugoslavia//Narodna Radinost Beograd."
Slovenian Couple (Dolls on right): 8in (20cm); silk mask faces with embroidered features; cotton over armature body; white felt hands; man has hand-loomed cotton, embroidered shirt; black

felt pants; red cord on doll is attached to a hand-loomed striped bag; black felt knicker-type pants; black yarn stockings; leather shoes made by braiding strips of leather together; Oriental upturned pointed shoes; Woman wears hand-loomed white blouse and vari-colored striped, pleated skirt; red felt weskit with sequins and gold thread closings; black embroidered apron; same upturned leather

shoes as man; late 1950s.
MARKS: "865A Slovenia" tag for both dolls.
SEE: *Illustration 249*, page 157. *Lois Janner Collection.*

Chimney Sweep: 7in (18cm); made of fired clay over armature of metal; metal hands and ladder; carries ladder and metal scraper on long wire chain; from the town of Kranj in Slovenia; 1974.

Many other countries including France made *Chimney Sweep* dolls. These were supposed to be good luck charms.
MARKS: "Kranj" printed on bottom of stand.
SEE: *Illustration 250.*, page 157. *Louise Schnell Collection.*

Price Guide

#	Description	Price
1	Sasha. Very rare doll.	not enough sample prices.

AUSTRIA

#	Description	Price
2	Mozart	$65-85
2	Helga	$10-15
2	Mozart's Sister	$65-85
3	Tyrolean Boy (Doll on right)	$400-450
3	Tyrolean Boy (Doll on left)	$15-20
4	Leni	$50-70
4	Whistling Franzl	$60-80
4	Lady in Black Dress	$60-80
5	Innsbrook Dancing Couple (both dolls)	$40-50
6	Vienna Lady	$40-60

AZORES

#	Description	Price
7	Azores Man	$30-40
7	Azores Lady	$30-40

BELGIUM

#	Description	Price
8	Lady with Milk Pail	$25-35
9	Liberated Belgium	$65-85
10	Lang Soldier	$275-325
10	Belgian Lacemaker	$15-20
10	Flandre Sailor	$30-40

BULGARIA

#	Description	Price
11	Bulgarian Man	$35-45
11	Bulgarian Woman	$35-45
12	Dancing Bulgarian Girl	$30-40 in original box
12	Palm Sunday in Bulgaria	$85-100
12	Dancing Bulgarian Boy	$30-40 in original box

CZECH REPUBLIC AND SLOVAKIA

#	Description	Price
13	Pizen Girl	$35-50
14	Tatra Boy	$25-35
14	Tatra Girl	$25-35
15	Moravian Girl	$50-60
16	Kojovijan Boy	$25-35
16	Kojovijan Girl	$25-35
17	Piestany Dolls (From left to right)	$30-40 / $60-75 / $25-35 / $70-80 / $75-100
18	Czech Doll with Crown	$150-175
18	Czech Doll with Red Print Headdress	$50-60

#	Description	Price
19	(From left to right)	$70-80 / $20-30 / $85-100 / $30-40 / $40-50
20	Borsice-venec Girl	$50-75
20	Girl with Red Printed Headdress	$50-75
21	Olsava Couple	$70-80 both
21	Bartered Bride	$55-75
21	Boy	$55-75
22	Old Czechoslovakian Doll	$125-150
23	Copenhagen Girl	$600-700
24	Girl from Mor	$18-25
25	Amager Island Girl	$15-20
25	Doll from Dragor	$30-35
26	Danish Nissi	$20-25 each
27	Copenhagen Mother and Baby	$35-45
28	Boy in Danish Costume	$5-7
28	Danish Soldier with Gun	$10-15
28	Peter Wessel	$30-35

ENGLAND

#	Description	Price
29	Corn Maiden	$15-20
29	Bobbin Doll	$15-20
30	Pearlie Lady	$50-75
31	Empress of England Sailor	$12-15
31	Tower Guard	$15-20
31	English Bobby (Policeman)	$30-35
32	Clothespin Dolls	$5-20
33	Grenadier Foot Guard	$600-700
33	Small Grenadier Foot Guard	$20-25
34	Queen Elizabeth I	$100-125 (bisque)
34	Queen Elizabeth II	$100-125 (bisque)
34	Queen Victoria	$100-125 (bisque)
35	King Edward VIII	not enough sample prices
35	King George VI	$500-700
36	Yeoman of the Guard	$100-125+
36	John Bull	$140-160 very few prices available
37	Penny Wooden	$15-25
37	Old Cottage Scottish Soldier	$130-160+
38	Dean's Golliwog	$100-120

159

Illus. #	Description	Price
	ESTONIA	
39	Estonian Girl	$125-150
	FINLAND	
40	Finnish Eskimo Baby	not enough sample prices
41	Finnish Boy	$20-25
41	Finnish Girl	$20-25
42	Marta Finnish Girl	$100-125
	FRANCE	
43	Doll from Quimper	$150-200
44	Girl from Quiberon	$50-55
45	Baby Babig-Koant	$200-250
46	Girl from Benodeten	$35-50
47	French Lisieux Candy Container	$100-125
47	Pont-Aven Brittany Girl	$190-225
48	Ma Normandie Poupes	$35-50
49	Justine of St. Lo	$40-60
50	Marie Antoinette	$20-30
50	King Louis XVI	$20-30
51	Raynal Nobility Girl and Boy	$1600-1800 pair
52	Ravca Fisherman	$150-200
52	Ravca Pedlar Woman	$300-350
53	Thumette of Pont l'Abbe	$125-150
54	Girl from Gascogne	$20-30
54	Member of Nobility	$30-35
54	Girl from Champagne	$30-35
54	Girl from Boulogne	$15-20
54	Girl from Toulouse	$15-20
55	Girl from Alsace-Lorraine	$800-900
56	Pas de Calais	$300-350
57	Lanternier Provincial Girl	$625-650
58	Poupees Venus from Arles	$700-900
59	Bernadette Doll	$150-200
60	Sardane Dancers	no available price
61	Sardane Dancing Festival	no price
62	Girly from Lyon	$10-15
63	Girl from Nice	$15-20
63	Girl from Cannes	$15-25
64	Brittany or Normandy Boy	$100-150
65	Mother with Cradle	$45-60
65	Man with Bed Warmer	$45-60
66	Journey of the Santons	$5-10 for each small figure
67	Santon Painter	$50-100
68	Champenoise Doll (Right)	$50-75
68	Champenoise Doll (Left)	$50-75
69	Provence Girl	$300-350
69	Raynel Provence Girl	$650-750
69	Provence Girl	$100-125

Illus. #	Description	Price
	GERMANY	
70	Munich Woman	$60-70
70	Heidelberg Woman	$35-45
71	Luneberger-Heide Region girl	$25-30
71	Luneberger-Heide Shepherd	$20-25
71	Franken Madchen Girl	$35-45
71	Gura Marburg	$75-100
71	Stoll Puppen Harz	$25-30
72	Lubeck Testorf Region Lady	$20-25
72	Child from Nordfriesland	$20-25
72	Child from Vierlanden-Hamburg	$20-25
72	Lady from Hamburg Fish Market	$35-45
73	German Peasant Gretchen	$180-220
73	Bavarian Boy	$700-800
74	Pied Piper of Hamlin	$25-30
74	Christkind	$20-30
75	Goose Girl	$100-125 original in plastic container
76	Red Riding Hood and Huntsman	$200-250 pair
77	Hansel, Gretel, Witch (set)	$20-25
78	Small Hesse Doll	$30-40
78	Large Hesse Doll	$125-175
79	Hesse Doll (Middle)	$125-150
79	Key Wind Hesse Doll	$35-50
79	Hesse Doll (Left)	$100-125
80	Black Forest Region Doll	$125-150
80	Bordensee Region Doll	$75-100
81	Girl from Spreewald	$20-30
81	Girl from Helgoland	$18-25
81	Leipzinger Messe MM	$20-25
81	Girl from Schlesien	$25-30
81	Girl from Monschau Eiffel	$20-25
81	Markgraflerland Girl	
81	Helgoland Man	$25-30
81	Pommern	$16-20
81	Pommern Girl	$16-30
82	Wassau Doll (Right)	$30-40
82	Wassau Doll (Left)	$30-40
83	Olympic Doll	$100-150 mint in box
83	Gura Bavarian Girl	$75-100
84	Monk of Munchen (Munich)	$25-30
85	Hofbrau House Squeaker	$35-45
86	Bavarian Boy	$30-35
86	Garmisch Girl	$30-35
87	Bodensee Doll	$800-900
87	Blonde Bisque Girl	$800-1200

GREECE

Illus. #	Description	Price
88	Greek Woman (Left)	$35-45
88	Sheep Herder (Middle)	$35-45
88	Young Sheep Herder (Right)	$35-45
89	Zarkos (Soldier)	$40-50 in original box with papers
89	Girl with Spindle	$25-35
90	Man (Left)	$75-85
90	Lady with Striped Blouse	$75-85
90	Lady from Lesbos	$75-85
90	Lady with Embroidered Apron	$75-85
91	Crete Man	$75-85
91	Lady	$75-85
91	Chios Man	$75-85
91	Mykonos Lady	$75-85
91	Crete Man Dancer	$75-85

GREENLAND

Illus. #	Description	Price
140	Greenland Doll	$40-50

HUNGARY

Illus. #	Description	Price
92	Marga Mother	$200-400 depending on size and embroidery
92	Marga Baby	$75-100
93	Hungarian Bride	$30-40
93	Small Marga Doll	$40-50+ very few prices available
93	Hungarian Bridegroom	$35-40
94	Hungarian Girl with Wreath	$30-40
95	Hungarian Dancing Man	$40-55
95	Hungarian Dancing Woman	$40-55
96	Baba Hungarian Man	$60-75
97	Budapest Girl	$125-175 few prices available.

ICELAND

Illus. #	Description	Price
98	Iceland Girl	$40-50
99	Iceland Girl	$150-175

IRELAND

Illus. #	Description	Price
100	1735 Replica Doll	no price available.
101	Packie (Patrick)	$45-65
101	Sewing Lady Mother	$75-100
102	Irish Bisque Pair	$575-600 for pair
103	Flower Seller of Dublin	$50-65
103	Aran Fisherman	$50-65
104	Celtic Toy Fisherman	$10-15
105	Mollye the Emigrant	$40-50
106	Brogues and Stockings	no price available
107	Leprechaun	How can you price a Leprechaun?
108	Irish Harpist	$30-40
109	Donegal Man	$75-100
110	Connemara Farm Woman	$25-30
110	Connemara Woman and Donkey	$45-55
110	Jay Irish Nun	$50-65
111	Sligo Woman	$50-65
112	Bisque Irish Doll	$225-250
175	Crolly Doll	$25-35
175	Irish Girl in Red Cape	$25-30

ITALY

Illus. #	Description	Price
113	Friuli Doll	$15-20
113	Sardinian Doll	$200-250
113	Siciliana Doll	$65-75
114	Castelrotto Girl	$350-450+
115	Palio Flag Bearer	$35 complete with stand and pamphlet
116	Venice Carnival Lady	$35-50
116	Harlequin in Music Box	$50-60
117	Eros Gondolier	$20-30
117	Lenci Gondolier	$50-60
118	Lenci Cortina D'Ampezzo (Lenci)	$200-400
119	Girl from Valsarentino (Lenci)	$50-75
119	Girl from Calabria (Lenci)	$50-75
119	Girl from Sardegna (Lenci)	$50-75
120	Pulcinello Clown	$20-25
120	Colombina Clown	$20-25
121	Napoli Lady	$30-40
121	Sorrento Lady	$20-25
121	Lady from Island of Capri	$20-25
122	Magis Milano Girl	$25-30
122	Lenci Milano Girl	$300-350+
123	Swiss Guard with Helmet	$40-50
123	Swiss Guard with Beret	$20-25
123	Swiss Guard with No Hat	$15-20
123	E.N.A.P.L. Swiss Guard	$80-100
124	Magis Chubby Roman Couple (left)	$200-250 rare
124	Lenci Vinyl Doll	$100-125
124	Cloth Lady	
124	Lenci Roma Doll	$300-350+
124	Magis Roma Doll	$60-75

Illus. #	Description	Price
125	S.A.G.T. Florence Doll	$15-20
125	Lenci Florence Doll	$325-375
125	Lela Florence Doll	$25-30
126	Florence Watering Can Girl	$15-19
126	Italian Trumpeter	$20-25
127	Genova Lady	$15-20
127	Ventimiglia (Liguria) Lady	$15-20
128	Naples Couple	$100-150 pair
128	Naples Old Lady	$50-70
128	Magis Sardinian Lady	$50-65
129	Sorrento Man with Guitar	$25-30
130	Romeo and Juliet	$20-25 pair
131	Lenci Sardinian Girl	$600-800
132	Lenci Sicily Doll	$300-350+
133	Lenci Savoy Boy	$550-700+
133	Lenci Mountain Soldier	$500-600
134	Isotie Carabinieri	$150-200
134	Lenci Miniature Carabinieri	$450-600+
135	Vechiotti-Milano Lady	$100-125

SAN MARINO

Illus. #	Description	Price
136	San Marino Girl	$15-20
137	Roberto from San Marino	$20-25
138	San Marino Archer	$25-35+
138	Pisa (Tuscany)	$20-25
175	Sicily Girl	$35-45

LAPLAND

Illus. #	Description	Price
139	Greenland Doll	$40-50
139	Norwegian Laplander Man	$175-200
139	Lapland Boy	$15-20
139	Lapland Girl	$15-20
140	Swedish Lapland Boy	$175-200
141	Lapland Couple	$40-60
142	Norwegian Lapland Boy	$15-20
142	Swedish Laplander	$150-175
143	Lapland Boy on Skis	$50-75

LATVIA

Illus. #	Description	Price
144	Latvian Doll	$10-15

LITHUANIA

Illus. #	Description	Price
145	Lithuanian Dolls	$50-75 each

MADEIRA

Illus. #	Description	Price
146	Madeira Girl	$20-25

MALTA

Illus. #	Description	Price
147	Chetta from Malta	$30-35

MONACO

Illus. #	Description	Price
148	Monaco Soldier	$10-20

THE NETHERLANDS (HOLLAND)

Illus. #	Description	Price
149	Netherlands Regional Dolls	$50-75 very few sample prices
150	Netherland Regional Dolls	(see previous price)
151	Zuid-Beveland Girl	$175-195
151	Marken Fairy Tale Hat Girl	$235-265
152	Voldendam Couple	$235-265 each
153	Voldendam Dovina Girl	$75-85
154	Zuid-Veveland Man	$45-60
154	Edi Dutch Doll	$50-65
155	Delft Queen	$50-75
156	Dutch Sailor Smoking a Pipe	$200-225
157	Hera Girl	$85-100
157	Nederland Olanda Boy	$40-60
157	Hera Boy	$85-100
175	Dutch Girl	$15-20

NORWAY

Illus. #	Description	Price
158	Silk Scarf	no sample prices
159	Nissi, Ronnaug Petterssen	$500-600+ rare
160	Romsdal Girl	$60-70
160	Vest Agder Girl	$25-30
161	Hardanger Girl	$600-650+
162	Bisque Hardanger Girl	$300-400+
162	Old Swiss Guard	$300-400+
163	Norway Girl in White Dress	$20-25
163	Small Norway Girl	$15-20
164	Trolls	$40-50 each
165	Norwegian Bunad Paper Dolls	$30-35
166	Lillihammer Woodsman	$30-40
167	Setesdal Couple	$150-175 pair
168	Hallingdal Boy and Girl, Ronnaug Petterssen	$1200-1400 pair
168	Setesdal Girl	$50-75
169	Hardanger Boy, Ronnaug Petterssen	$80-90
169	Lom Village Girl	$25-35
169	Rattvik Boy	$75-125

POLAND

Illus. #	Description	Price
170	Polish Girl Washing Dishes	$35-40
170	Poland Man in Horse Costume	$40-55
171	King Zygmund August	$70-80
171	Queen Barbara Radziwell	$70-80
172	Dickinson as Spy (not a doll)	
173	Advertisement (no prices)	
174	Mountain Man and Bride	$200-225 pair
175	Polish Girl	$50-65

Illus. #	Description	Price
176	Spring Custom Polish Dolls ..	$40-45
177	Krakow Girl with Wreath	$85-125
177	Krakow Girl with Square Headdress	$40-45
178	Lalki Region Girl	$20-25
179	Polish Bagpiper	$100-125
175	Doll in Red Cape	no price available
186	Polish Peasant Woman	$95-125

PORTUGAL

Illus. #	Description	Price
180	Maria Helena Girl with Book	$15-30 depending on costume
181	Portugal Farm Couple...........	$20-35 each
182	Musical Couple	$25-30 pair
182	Girl with 7 Petticoats	$10-15
182	Fisherman from Nazare	$20-25

ROMANIA

Illus. #	Description	Price
183	Vlaska Girl.............................	$50-75
184	Man in Sheepskin Coat..........	$50-75
184	Man with Bagpipe	$50-75
184	Lady Carrying Jar	$50-75
184	Lady with Bag	$50-75
185	Rumanian Gypsy	$150-175
186	5 Antique dolls.....................	not enough sample prices
187	Rumanian Dancing Man	$35-45
188	Rumanian Bride	$150-175
188	Constanza Lady	$50-75

RUSSIA AND THE SOVIET UNION

Illus. #	Description	Price
189	Old Tea Cozy	$135
189	New Tea Cozy	$30-40
190	Soviet Union Girl	$25-35
190	Soviet Union Boy	$25-35
190	Ski Girl	$75-90
191	Russian Boyar Doll	$200-250
192	Russian Bride........................	$200-250
192	Russian Bridegroom	$200-250
193	Lady from Smolensk	
194	Russian Boy	$75-85
195	Uzbechka Boy	$50-65
195	Belorussia Lady	$65-85
195	Lady in Red and Yellow	$195
196	Nesting Dolls 1909	not enough sample prices
197	Nesting Dolls 1939	not enough sample prices

Illus. #	Description	Price
198	Nesting Siberian Dolls	$5-10
198	Nesting Ural Mountains Dolls	$7-10
198	Nesting Ukrainian Dolls	$39-50
198	Nesting Brest Dolls................	$15-20
198	Nesting Yashkar Dolls	$7-10
199	Czar and Family Nesting Dolls	$300
200	2 Soviet Boys	$175-225 each
201	Kirowz Man	$100-125
201	Mordwa Woman	$50-65
202	Russian Smoking Doll	$25-35
202	Ukraine Man	$20-30
203	Lady with High Hat	
203	Doll Sitting Down	
186	Russian Peasant	not enough sample prices
272	Ukranian Man	not enough sample prices

SCOTLAND

Illus. #	Description	Price
204	Barleycorn Scottish Doll	$20-25
205	Sheena Macleod Fishwife......	$50-85 depending on figure
206	Ilse Ludeke Bagpiper	$50-75
206	Scottish Liberty of London	$85-100
206	Small Bagpiper	$60-70
207	Keywind Scotsman	$40-50
207	Cloth Scottish Man	$40-50
207	Steiner Bisque Scottish girl ...	$175-200
207	Hewitt and Leadbeater	$150-175
207	Scottish Lady in Green	$30-40
37	Old Cottage Soldier	$135-165

SPAIN

Illus. #	Description	Price
208	Marriage Contract	$500-600 for set
209	Spanish Googly Lenci	$3000-3300 few sample prices
210	Gallegos Boy	$350-450+
211-213	Catalog Pages	no prices
214	Flamingo Female Dancer	$35-45
214	Flamingo Male Dancer	$25-35
215	Gypsy Playing Violin	$60-80
216	Catalonian Man	$45-55
216	Segovian Girl	$45-56
217	Matador................................	$100-125
217	Ferdinand the Bull	$175-200
218	Male N.A.T.I. Spanish Dancer...................................	$145-175

Illus. #	Description	Price
219	Klumpe Matador and Bull	$145-165
220	Andalusian Dancer	$150-175
222	Lagerterana Woman	$55-75
222	Badajoz Girl	$50-75
223	Gaucho from Zamorano	$150-200+
223	Zamorano Girl	$150-200+
224	Segoviano Man	$65-70
224	Segoviano Woman	$65-70
225	Spanish Woman	$200-225
225	Spanish Girl in Gold Dress	$125-150
226	Canary Island Dancing Couple	$30-45 each
227	Layna Girl with Straw Hat	$40-60
227	Layna Girl in Cowboy Suit	$40-60

SWEDEN

228	Sveg Girl	$15-20
228	Viking	$20-25
228	Oland Girl	$15-20
229	Leksand Dalarna Girl	$15-20
229	Leksand Dalarna Man	$15-20
230	Bride from Osterlen	$50-60
230	Peasant Girl	$15-18
230	Tailor	$75-85
231	Swedish Classroom	$300-350 for set
232	Peddler from Blekinge	$50-60
233	Gripsholm Sailor	$200-225
234	Skane Boy with Violin	$50-60

SWITZERLAND

235	Swiss Sheepherder	$45-50
236	Joanna from Lugano	$30-35
237	Alpine Girl	$60-80
237	Alpine Boy	$60-80

Illus. #	Description	Price
237	St. Bernard	$90-100
238	Inner Rhoden Appenzell Lady	$125-150
239	Bing Ausser Rhoden Appenzell Girl	$350-400
239	Bing Ausser Rhoden Appenzell Boy	$350-400
240	Girl from Vaud	$20-25
240	Austria Wachau Girl	$20-25
241 and 242	Bucherer Mountain Man	$200-225 from Swiss costumed doll
243	Bern Lady (left)	$350-400
243	Bern Lady (right)	$425-475
244	Swiss Man	$20-25
244	Swiss Woman	$20-25

WALES

245	Nora Wellings Wales Lady	$50-75
246	Myfanny (My Rare One)	$35-40 in box

YUGOSLAVIA

247	Slovenian Man	$125-150
247	Slovenian Woman	$125-150
248	Girl from Ljubljana	not enough sample prices
249	Yugoslavian Couple	$35-50 each
249	Croation Lady	$35-50
249	Slovenian Couple	$35-50 each
260	Chimney Sweep	25-35

Index

165

About the Authors

Both mother and daughter enjoy collecting dolls and learning more about dolls as a team. It was under-standable that their research efforts and their love of sharing doll information would progress from writing articles for the leading doll collector's magazines to a book. Their first book, *Hard Plastic Dolls, Volume I*, and the hundreds of letters of encouragement that they received started them on a dozen year odyssey of writing a total of seven books. Both skilled researchers, Polly says "It just came 'naturally' that my daughter, Pam, and I write about the hobby we enjoy so much—doll collecting."

A retired junior high school teacher and Coordinator for Chapter I Reading Program for the Wickliffe City Schools, Polly devotes most of her time to writing. Pam currently teaches fifth graders and is a performing harpsichordist with a Masters in Musicology. Both women reside in Ohio.